Our Stories

A Fiction Workshop for Young Authors

Other Clarion Books by Marion Dane Bauer

ABOUT WRITING

A Writer's Story
What's Your Story?

NOVELS

A Taste of Smoke
Face to Face
A Dream of Queens and Castles
Touch the Moon
On My Honor
Rain of Fire
Shelter from the Wind

Our Stories

A Fiction Workshop for Young Authors

COMPILED AND WITH COMMENTARY BY
Marion Dane Bauer

CLARION BOOKS / NEW YORK

Clarion Books
a Houghton Mifflin Company imprint
215 Park Avenue South, New York, NY 10003
Text copyright © 1996 by Marion Dane Bauer
All students' stories and story excerpts used by permission.

Type is 12/15 New Baskerville
Book design by Carol Goldenberg

For information about this and other Houghton Mifflin trade and refer-
ence books and multimedia products, visit The Bookstore at Houghton
Mifflin on the World Wide Web at (http://www.hmco.com/trade/).
Printed in the USA

Library of Congress Cataloging-in-Publication Data
Bauer, Marion Dane.
Our stories: a fiction workshop for young authors / by Marion Dane Bauer
         p.   cm.
Summary: This follow-up to What's Your Story? presents a selection of
short fiction written by students in grades four through twelve followed by
Bauer's comments on each.
ISBN 0-395-81598-3 PA ISBN 0-395-81599-1
1. Short story—Juvenile literature.   2. Fiction—Authorship—
Juvenile literature.   3. Child authors.   [1. Fiction—Authorship.
2. Creative writing.]   I. Title.
PN3373.B245 1996
808.3'1—dc2   95-51091
CIP   AC

BP 10 9 8 7 6 5 4 3

For young authors everywhere

Contents

Foreword

This book showcases some fine fiction by young writers. More important, though, it offers a workshop-style format that can help other developing writers improve their own story-writing skills.

The only way to learn to write is by writing. But writing can be a lonely occupation and one for which meaningful feedback is in short supply. So you write and write and write. How do you know when your stories are working? How do you learn what you can do to make them better?

The most effective way for most writers to learn to improve their stories is to be part of a workshop. A workshop is a gathering in which writers share their work with one another, offering support and suggestions for revisions. But unless such a workshop has a knowledgeable leader, it can easily descend into an "I'll-like-your-story-if-you-like-mine" situation or, worse, into an experience of criticism without support. And then no one learns and grows.

What I am offering here is a workshop on paper. You can't, of course, bring your story to this book for a critique. What you can do, however, is participate in evaluating other writers' stories, even step into those stories and try your own revisions from time to time. Then you can take what you have learned back to your own work.

The stories that are presented here were gathered over a period of two years. Most came through teachers who were working with my earlier book *What's Your Story? A Young Person's Guide to Writing Fiction* in their classrooms. Some came directly to me from young writers who had read *What's Your Story?* on their own and wanted to show me what they had done with it, or through contacts I have made at young authors' conferences and schools. A few others arrived through one of my adult students who wanted to share the work of gifted young writers.

I began this project with hundreds of manuscripts, grocery sacks full. I have ended with thirty. The stories you will find here were chosen because their authors did something especially well. They were also chosen because they gave me an opportunity to discuss some aspect of story writing for other developing writers to consider.

Probably none of these stories is yet ready for publication on its own merits. Fine writing, especially fiction writing, requires depth of life experience as well as talent. You will note that many of these writers were in elementary school when they wrote their stories. The talent is here. The life experience will come.

With the exception of standardizing spelling, punctuation, and paragraphing, correcting an occasional grammatical error, and cutting to meet space requirements, I have made no alterations in this work. Intruding an editor's hand would have been too easy, and I didn't want to lose the freshness of these young writers' voices.

I thank everyone who presented stories to me, students and teachers alike. I only wish I could have used more of what I was given. I also thank Kimberly Nightingale, teacher and writer, who helped in the process of reading and making the first round of manuscript selections. And, as always, I am grateful to my life partner, Ann Goddard, whose comments and support are invaluable through the gathering of every one of my books, and my editor, James Cross Giblin, who has been there from the beginning.

Though I believe *Our Stories: A Fiction Workshop for Young Authors* can stand alone as an exploration of fiction-writing techniques, the discussions of craft this book presents are not intended to be complete. Rather, *Our Stories* is meant to be a companion to *What's Your Story? A Young Person's Guide to Writing Fiction*, which explores issues of craft more fully, and *A Writer's Story: From Life to Fiction*, which focuses on the role of inspiration in the writing of fiction.

I congratulate all whose stories appear here. I am certain we will hear more from some of these writers in the years to come. And I hope many more young authors will be helped to discover their own best stories through this workshopping process.

Write on!

CHAPTER 1

From the Beginning

Writing the opening lines of a story is a bit like starting to ski at the steepest part of a hill. You must have all your skills under control from the first instant. Balancing the demands of a strong beginning is a particularly difficult task for developing writers. I have often thought it a shame that we can't just begin our stories in the middle. Then we could return to deal with the problems presented by the beginning after the story is under control.

Most writers, however, myself included, feel compelled to begin at the beginning. So let's face the difficulties of writing the opening lines of our stories straight on.

A strong beginning is essential. Without that, you will not lure readers into your story. And luring readers is every story's first task.

Your beginning must let readers know what kind of story to expect: a fairy tale, a romance, a ghost story, a realistic drama, or one of the many other possibilities.

The opening paragraphs of your story must also give your readers basic information: who is the story about,

1

where is it set, when is it taking place, and what is the main character's problem? That last, *what is the problem?*, is the most important piece of information. The problem provides the narrative hook that will capture readers and draw them into your story. Much of the rest of the necessary information can come along more slowly. If readers don't encounter some kind of problem very quickly, however, they are apt to quit reading. Most won't realize that a *problem* is what they are missing. They will simply decide that the story is "boring."

One of my adult writing students once came up with an opening line I have always remembered. "There were three people in the church, but only two of them had guns." That catches your attention, doesn't it? The hook is certainly there, though there is a great deal we don't yet know. The task of the writer, then, would be to follow up this strong opening with an equally strong story.

Strong opening lines are not difficult to come up with. The challenge is to move smoothly from those opening lines into your story. Take note of the way this untitled story, written by a young writer, begins:

I was running. As fast as I could, I was running from them. My parents. How could they do this to me? They took everything—my friends, school, parties, shopping, boys—they took it away.

My name is SaraAnn Larson. I'm fifteen and I just got my driver's permit. It was around the same time when the PROBLEM started.

Having parents who are artists and writers is bad enough, but having parents who suddenly decide we should buy a farm, move out to the country and start homeschooling is awful.

Like I said, the problem started a couple of months ago. My parents were acting real weird, asking my ten-year-old sister and me what we thought of farms and the country and homeschool. I thought homeschool was okay—I had had a couple of friends leave school to start it—but not for me. I'm too outgoing, friendly, social to start staying home and doing my work there. So you can imagine the shock I felt when two weeks ago my parents informed me that they had bought a farm complete with three horses, two cows, four pigs, and dozens of chickens.

They had expected me to be happy because I had once remarked how much fun it would be to stay on a farm—for a vacation, NOT to live—and needless to say I was not thrilled. I had burst into tears. Naturally, a fight burst out soon afterwards. I couldn't believe what they had done. They couldn't believe I was acting so childish. They were taking away everything, turning me into a prisoner. My parents' reasons for it were dull, boring, and they did not change my mind. They said it would be fun, educational, and I would meet new people.

"Where?" I had shouted. They never answered that one.

The next day at cheerleading practice, I loaded up on my friends' sympathy, but that didn't help much.

I had tried everything in my power to stay, even locking myself in the bathroom on moving day, but nothing worked. They just took a coat hanger and picked the lock. I wish they were criminals. Then we would have had a chance to stay in the city.

I would rather walk on a hard concrete sidewalk

than a dirt road. I would rather look at skyscrapers than trees. I would rather live anywhere than nowhere, which was where I was living now.

My sister, Marie, was crazy about moving. She told everyone, including strangers.

I can see my parents' views, sort of. New York had too much crime, pollution, and people to feel comfortable—to them, anyway. That's the problem with artists. They need a lot of space.

The farmhouse was okay. Large and airy, it was better than any apartment we have ever lived in.

My parents gave me a choice of the bedrooms first. They probably thought that would make me feel better. I took the room that my parents had said earlier would make a great studio. But I still hadn't wanted to move.

So that's why I was running. Running anywhere. Running away. At least I knew I wouldn't get kidnapped or murdered out here. Our neighbors probably didn't even know what the word murder meant. . . .

Brooke Roberts
Grade 8
Homeschool
St. Paul, Minnesota

Brooke's instinct in opening her story with the character's problem right up front is a very good one. We not only understand SaraAnn's problem, but we are immediately involved in her struggle as she sets out to solve it. Few fifteen-year-old girls would feel happy about such a total change in lifestyle, especially when given no control over the decisions being made. And running away is serious action that demands a reader's attention.

Brooke shows that she has a good understanding of

her characters. The description of the parents "acting weird," asking SaraAnn and her sister "what we thought of farms and the country and homeschool," rings true. I can imagine her parents leading up to the topic of moving in exactly such a way. The idea of the younger sister being so crazy about the idea that "she told everyone, including strangers" reveals a lot about the sister, too. And when SaraAnn, given the choice of bedrooms, chooses the room she knew her parents wanted as a studio, I can feel the tension in that family, can feel SaraAnn's anger, and can even guess at her parents' frustration.

There is a problem here, however. Despite the very active beginning with SaraAnn running away, the story movement stops completely in the second paragraph. The narrator interrupts her own story to explain the situation, and during the explanation, readers are distanced from the opening action. In fact, I think many will be surprised to find SaraAnn still running after nearly two pages of explanation.

I asked Brooke if she would consider rewriting her story's opening for me. I suggested that she start, this time, with an argument between SaraAnn and her parents. She could reveal her main character's problem that way without so much explanation. This was the new opening she wrote.

I was running. As fast as I could, I was running. From my parents. How could they do this to me? They took away everything—my friends, school, parties, shopping—they took it away. So that's why I was running.

Everything started to go wrong last month when my mom and dad decided that the stress of city life was affecting their artistic abilities. So they bought a small farm in the middle of nowhere (the closest neighbors are a mile away), complete with four pigs, three horses, two cows, and dozens of chickens.

Yesterday was the day we moved.

I woke up this morning in an awful mood. Thumping down the stairs and into the large, fifties-style kitchen, I found my mom dancing around the kitchen, singing along with the radio and making waffles.

Mom stopped dancing when I stepped into the room.

"Good morning," she said, turning off the music.

"It is not a good morning, and why are you so perky?" I grumbled.

"You watch your mouth, young lady! And I'm *perky* because it's so refreshing waking up in the morning to see the sun rise and hear the birds sing. It's wonderful. And," she added, "if you had woken up earlier, you would have seen it too. It's almost eleven."

"I hate it here," I said loudly.

"Oh, now stop that. It's the best for everyone. Make the best of it. Oh, and if you go into the woods today remember to stay on the paths. There's over twenty square miles out there, and we don't want you to get lost."

"The only place I'm going is home," I told her.

"Morning," my father said, striding in and grabbing an apple off the kitchen table. He was followed by my nine-year-old sister, Lisa.

"Going out to feed the chickens, Mom!" she yelled as she ran through the kitchen and out the back door.

"Where's the waffle maker?" Mom asked Dad, giving him a kiss.

"In a box somewhere," he replied, turning to give me a hug. He stopped when he noticed my scowling face.

"What's wrong?" he asked, looking from me to Mom and back again.

"I do not want to stay here. I hate it here," I told him.

"SaraAnn, just think of it! I can work on my writing without city noise and Mom can work on her paintings wherever she wants."

I was getting angry. "Everything is for you! You, you, you!" . . .

And the argument continues, escalating until, finally, with no other solution in sight, SaraAnn decides to run away.

This draft could still use further work, but Brooke is on the right track. Notice how much information we get through the argument between SaraAnn and her parents. We find out that the family has just moved, that SaraAnn hates the farm they have moved to, that her parents and younger sister are happy with it, that her father is a writer and her mother an artist. We even get a hint about the difficulties SaraAnn will face if she does decide to run away when her mother warns her against getting lost. And if I had given you more of the argument, there would have been more important discoveries, all of which come through the angry confrontation between SaraAnn and her parents.

Because Brooke obviously loved her original opening—"I was running. As fast as I could, I was running"—she has held on to that, although she was willing to make other substantial changes. I would suggest, though, that her opening paragraph presents the same difficulty it did in her first draft. Too much takes place before we get back to SaraAnn's decision to run away. If I were to work with Brooke further on this story, I would recommend that, in the next draft, she drop the opening paragraph entirely.

The most difficult task every writer faces is having to cut words we love. However, letting go of lines and paragraphs and pages that don't work is always the best way to serve our stories. This story would be stronger if the running away appeared in its natural order and the story opened with what is now the second paragraph.

If Brooke's story began with "Everything started to go wrong last month when my mom and dad decided that the stress of city life was affecting their artistic abilities," we would be introduced quickly to the story problem. But that opening doesn't feel as strong as the running away, does it? That is because it is explanation, not action.

What if the story opened instead with "I woke up this morning in an awful mood"? In the next sentence the story moves into action and in the next paragraph into dialogue, strong dialogue in which the story's conflict is laid out. Without any of the previous explanation, the argument would need to be played out carefully to reveal very clearly what SaraAnn is unhappy about, but that wouldn't be difficult to do. The reader could then move forward without interruption to the moment when the main character decides to run away.

Another story, also untitled, opens with a more old-fashioned format. Behind this story is a traditional storyteller who, though never identified, is speaking directly to us. It begins like this:

Prologue

An old couple woke one morning to find a tiny bundle wrapped in a beautiful scarf on their doorstep. They took the baby girl in and named her Laraya. The girl grew to be a strong, cheerful person with black hair and surprising blue eyes staring out of her tan face. She wore the scarf she had been found in and often thought of her mysterious arrival, for her foster parents had kept nothing from her.

When Laraya was seven they died, and she was forced to wander in the streets, finding food however she could. She soon forgot her grief over the dead and was occupied with keeping herself alive. Another child might have died when faced with such a situation, but Laraya had a good character and was determined to live, besides. She soon joined a group of children like herself and learned from them, and they learned from her. And so Laraya grew up in the marketplace, laughing and skipping . . . and stealing just like any other child. This story opens six years after she was left without a home or guardian. . . .

Chapter One

It was a busy day in the marketplace. The merchants were out with a vengeance, vying with each other to praise their wares the best. The streets were crowded with people, from slaves and beggars and pickpockets in their dirty, off-white clothes to the nobles carried on silk-hung litters with guards and servants surrounding them.

A group of children sat huddled in a corner discussing what they were going to do that day. No one noticed them. Indeed, if they had, they would have said that they were up to no good. This was true. But they did have to eat, and "no good" was how they did it. Voices began to be discernible from the rest of the group.

"Hey, do you know what? There's a . . ."

"Shut up! I want to talk. There's . . ."

"Did you see?"

"I saw . . ."

"Guess what!"

"BE QUIET!" a voice roared. "Can't you tell a simple thing? Anyway, there's a great group on its way. They're not too fancy so that there are a lot of guards, but rich enough to get plenty. I think I'll try that stern-faced guy over there, toward the back. Now Koran, you're not that good, so why don't you try that lady over there. As for you . . ."

Pretty soon everybody was ready.

The children darted in at intervals, slipped a light hand into a pocket or purse, and were away. There was a bright flicker of color as their leader, Laraya, began to move. She was the best of them all and often chose people who looked hard. Suddenly her watchers caught their breath. Laraya's face turned pale as the man's strong hand clamped down on her wrist. Only once before had this happened. That time she had tricked the man into letting go of her. She knew that this man would not be tricked.

Behind her her band was aghast. The penalty for being caught stealing was being a slave for the person you stole from. And that man looked like one mean master.

Alder Brannin
Grade 6
Woodbury School
Shaker Heights, Ohio

Would you go on reading? I would. I want very much to learn what will happen to Laraya.

This story, too, opens with explanation, with a summation of the main character's history, a technique not often used in modern stories. The key here, however, is the word *modern*. Alder is not writing a modern story. She has chosen to use a more old-fashioned technique to fit her old-fashioned story, that of the invisible, omniscient (all-knowing) storyteller behind the story. If this were a modern story—one of a girl having to give up malls for a farm, for instance—such a technique would not serve the writer well. We readers might even grow impatient with it. This story has a folk quality, however, and is clearly set in a past that fits the folk nature of the telling. Thus, the summing up of the opening prologue seems more acceptable.

The hazard remains, though, that some readers might skip over the prologue, impatient to begin the story. So even in this case, the author might want to consider working Laraya's background into the story as it moves along instead of opening with a summation. We would need little or no background in this opening scene to keep us involved in the situation. All of that can come later. What we need to know here is that the main character, Laraya, is in charge of this group of children who are thieves, which we learn quickly.

Alder has done a number of things very well in these opening pages. She has chosen good details. Notice the description of Laraya and the appealing information that she was found wrapped in a beautiful scarf which she continued to wear. Then there are the dirty, off-white clothes of the slaves and beggars and pickpockets and "the bright flicker of color" as Laraya begins to move into the crowd. I especially liked the irony of the

11

line "And so Laraya grew up in the marketplace, laughing and skipping . . . and stealing just like any other child." And the final line of Chapter 1—"And that man looked like one mean master"—would compel any reader to turn the page.

Let's look at a story that uses more modern techniques, opening with action and no explanations at all.

Daddy's Little Girl

"Daddy, no!" I screamed, trying to back away from him. "Daddy, you're hurting me!"

I looked around the room trying to find an escape route. There was only one exit, and it was on the other side of the room. I had two plans of action: I could break free of my father and try to avoid the couch and love seat as I ran to the door. Or I could scream and hope the neighbors heard me. With my luck the neighbors wouldn't even be home.

I opened my mouth to scream but no sound was heard. I was trapped. There was no way of escaping my father.

"Please, Daddy! Let me go! I don't like this!" I pleaded, not knowing what he was going to do to me.

Amy Jackson
Grade 11
North Baltimore High School
North Baltimore, Ohio

We are drawn instantly into the main character's problem, aren't we? Our interest is captured even before we fully understand what that problem is. As the story moves on, Amy will need to give us more information, of course. Not just about what is going on in this particular moment, but also about the history that lies behind it. We will need to be able to understand both characters and the significance of what is happening between them.

"Daddy's Little Girl" is a contemporary story using modern storytelling techniques and using them very well. We are clearly inside the point of view of the main character, not seeing the world through an omniscient storyteller. And the story starts with action that reveals the story problem, not with explanation.

To return to Alder's story about Laraya, even though it is set in the past, the author could have told it in the same contemporary style both Amy and Brooke used. Alder's story works well as she has presented it. Still, rewriting the first chapter of her story using the more modern technique could be an interesting exercise.

Start off with Laraya, inside her. Look out at the market and at the other children through her eyes. How is she feeling? Is she hungry? Is she simply restless and wanting action? Is she worried about the other children? Who, specifically? Or is there someone in her group of young thieves she needs to prove herself to so that she can remain the leader? Because at this point we know Laraya only from the outside, the possibilities are nearly endless. Find Laraya's motive inside yourself. What reason for approaching these particular travelers feels right to you?

Once you decide upon Laraya's motive, begin writing just as the group of well-to-do people enters the square, and let us experience all that happens through Laraya. Let her look and hear and taste and touch. Climb inside her skin when the man she is trying to rob grabs her wrist. Record not only what she says to the other children but her thoughts and feelings as well. If you can become Laraya in the midst of such strong opening action, you will bring your readers right along with you.

We will have no choice but to go on reading.

What you will be doing in reworking this story opening is learning how to start your own stories off in the strongest way. At the same time, you will be practicing other important techniques. In just a few paragraphs, you will be learning to develop character, to move inside your main character's point of view, and to reveal your story through action. We will work with all of these techniques in the chapters to come.

Let's begin with action. Show, don't tell.

CHAPTER 2

Show, Don't Tell

" Tell me a story," we begged our mother or father when we were very young. And we all have a strong response to that remembered voice, weaving a tale. "Once upon a time" does more than signal the beginning of a story. It says, "All is well. I am here. You are cared for."

As we grow older, though, and turn to reading stories ourselves, our demands begin to change. We want our stories to be more than a form of comfort, a soothing lullaby sung by a familiar voice. We begin to demand to live our stories, to be challenged and excited and stretched. We learn to enjoy even fiction that frightens us or makes us feel sad. In fact, many of us seek out tales precisely for the tears they bring or the chill they send down the spine.

As a writer, though, it is much easier simply to *tell* your story than it is to draw your readers in so they can live the story events with and through your main character. Most beginning fiction writers, both young people and adults, have to work long and hard to learn the techniques that will make their stories come alive on the page.

15

When we dealt with beginnings in the last chapter, we also began to deal with the issue of telling. How easy it is to start a story by simply telling readers what they will need to know. It is easier to continue a story that way, too. But a story that is told is rarely as effective for readers as one that is shown or acted out.

Let's explore the issue further by examining another story by a young writer.

The Air Pie

There once was a boy named Jonathan and a little girl named Abby. They were brother and sister, and they lived on a small farm with their mother and father. Their farm was a lovely place to live. They had a small white house with green shutters. An old cow lived in the barn, and a dapple-gray horse stayed close to his favorite spot under a green apple tree. They had a dog and three cats that kept mice out of the barn. Six chickens pecked in the yard while one duck swam on the pond.

Jonathan was three years older than Abby, and Abby loved Jonathan very much. Everyone had chores to do, and everything went along very well until Jonathan had a problem. He did not like "wommin's" work. Jonathan decided he could get by without doing his share of the "wommin's" chores.

One day he was weeding the garden with his sister. Now if there was anything Jonathan hated, it was to weed the garden. That was definitely "wommin's" work! He was ten years old, and he was a "man." This particular day Jonathan decided that there was no way, no chance, no how he was going to do any more weeding, so he quit.

When Dad came out that evening to check the progress, the onion and bean rows Abby did looked fine, but the six rows of corn Jonathan was supposed to have weeded were hardly started. Dad called Jonathan for an explanation. Jonathan tried to explain his theory on "wommin's" work and that he wanted no more of it, but he soon found himself in the corn rows with the hoe! That was bad, but the worst thing was he had to miss a baseball game in town that he had been planning to see.

Abby went out to check Jonathan later, and she was sure she saw tears in his eyes. Now, Abby loved her brother, so she tried to help. It did seem to cheer Jonathan up a bit. They worked together quickly, and Jonathan was even able to catch the last few innings of the baseball game.

A few days later, Jonathan decided he liked gathering eggs even less than he liked weeding corn, so he talked Abby into doing it for him. Her chore was to put out corn for the chickens, and since there was a very mean old hen, Jonathan was to gather the eggs. Abby reluctantly agreed to do Jonathan's job.

Everything would have been fine if old Hazel, the hen, had not reached out and pecked Abby. She came running out of the hen house with three little bruises on her arm where Hazel had pecked her. Jonathan convinced Abby that if she told their mother he had not done his chores, he would be punished again. Abby, being loyal to her brother, kept her mouth shut. That evening Mother asked Abby about her arm. Abby told her she could not remember exactly what had happened. As Abby looked at Jonathan, he just looked away guiltily.

The next day was blackberry-picking day. Jonathan

17

and Abby were dressed for blackberry picking; they had on old clothes. Even though it was very hot, they had to wear long pants and long sleeves to keep the briars from snagging and scratching. They put their pants into their socks to keep out the chiggers, and they put on big hats to give them some shade. They headed down the road to the blackberry patch. Both children had shiny new buckets to put the juicy berries in.

As they left, Mom yelled to them that she would make each one his own special pie with the berries they picked. Were they happy to hear that! They were to have pie for dinner. Their very own pie! Both of them could almost taste the pies as they continued on their way to the blackberry patch.

It sure was hot that day. Jonathan did not want to pick blackberries, so he decided he would lie down under the big oak tree and rest while Abby went to the patch. Abby took Jonathan's shiny bucket with her. She worked very hard and soon was very hot. The mosquitoes were especially bad that day. The chiggers seemed to go right through her socks and chew on her ankles.

Abby toughed it out while Jonathan snoozed by the tree. Finally, both shiny buckets were full, and Abby came out of the patch. She looked very hot! She had some snags in her hair. As always, some briars had managed to find her arms even in the long sleeves. Her hands were stained with juice, but Abby knew how good that pie was going to taste.

As she walked by the oak tree Jonathan woke up and started to walk beside her. He took one shiny bucket to carry. When they reached home Mother welcomed them, looked them over really carefully and suggested they go for a swim in the creek. She then went into the kitchen to make the pies.

That evening at supper there was no need to tell Jonathan and Abby to finish their plates. They both did in nothing flat and sat waiting for their pies. Finally, the time came, and Mom set the long-awaited treats in front of the children. Abby took a bite of the pie and told Mother it was the best ever. Mother thanked Abby and told her how much she appreciated her help in picking the berries.

As Jonathan put his fork in the pie, he had a funny look on his face. He looked at Mother, and she smiled a big smile and asked how he liked his pie.

Jonathan looked over to his mom and said, "But Mom, there aren't any blackberries in my pie!"

Mom answered and said, "Yes, Jonathan. I said I would put all the blackberries you picked right there in your pie!"

And Jonathan knew she had done exactly that.

Gretchen Yancey
12th grade
Hannibal High School
Hannibal, Missouri

"The Air Pie" is a good story, well told. It builds nicely, using the three separate events that demonstrate Jonathan's decision not to do "wommin's" work and their growing consequences. The folksy tone fits the kind of story it is, too. I especially like "there was no way, no chance, no how he was going to do any more weeding." The phrase "'wommin's' work" has exactly

19

the kind of resonance the author intends. And the carefully chosen specifics in the opening description of the farm set the scene beautifully.

As a modern folktale, a variation on the classic "The Little Red Hen," "The Air Pie" is quite effective. The comeuppance Jonathan gets at the end for his laziness feels both appropriate and satisfying. My only suggestion, if we are content with having the story told, is that the ending would be stronger if the idea of "wommin's" work were brought in one last time and tied up with some final comment.

Having said that, however, let's consider what would happen to "The Air Pie" if it were rewritten to a more contemporary standard. What if the story were shown, not told?

The first decision we would need to make is a simple but important one. Whose story is it? With most stories, this decision is easy. The main character is the one who has the problem, the one who is struggling to bring about some change. As "The Air Pie" is written, the struggle belongs to Jonathan. (If it were written from Abby's point of view, she would have to struggle to get her brother to change instead of accepting the situation, as she does now.)

Let's decide, then, that Jonathan is the main character. The first step in preparing to revise the story will be to look inside Jonathan to discover who he is. What has prompted him to decide that he shouldn't be required to do "'wommin's' work"? Is he a dreamer with great plans for himself, plans that make much of the work on this small farm seem unimportant? Is he simply lazy, someone who doesn't like to get his hands dirty or to exert himself? Does he admire his father and see him as "above" the chores that are doled out to a ten-year-old boy? Maybe Jonathan's motives come from a mixture of these ideas or from something else entirely.

Once you have decided upon the reasons behind Jonathan's objections, you are ready to rewrite Gretchen's story in a more active style. If you were creating your own story from scratch, there would be many more steps to go through before you put down your first words. But in this case, Gretchen has done much of the work for you, so you can start right in.

What might the first lines of "The Air Pie" be like if you were to begin with action, with Jonathan struggling to solve his problem, rather than with a description of the family and the farm? Here is one possibility that I have played out:

Jonathan leaned on his hoe and gazed down the long row of corn. It was endless. And there were five more rows waiting when this one was done. "Wommin's work," he muttered, leaning more heavily on the hoe. The sun was a burning weight on his shoulders and back.

"What did you say?" Jonathan's younger sister, Abby, straightened up from the row of beans she was weeding and smiled in his direction. "Was you talking to me, Jon?"

"I said weeding is wommin's work," he said, more distinctly this time, "and I ain't doing it no more. No way, no chance, no how."

Abby's smile faded, and she glanced off toward the barn with a worried frown. "Goodness!" she said. "You better not let Daddy catch you talking like that."

But Jonathan just shook his head. Their father was a

21

man. You didn't see men weeding any old rows of corn. And wasn't Jonathan ten years old now? Surely he was a man, too.

Notice the amount of information the reader has gathered in those few lines, without any explanation at all. We know that Jonathan is the main character, because we are seeing the world through his eyes, sharing his thoughts. He is, moreover, clearly the one who has the problem, and he is ready to do something about it. We also know that he has a younger sister, Abby, and that his father, at least in Jonathan's perception, doesn't do "wommin's" work, which is the primary basis for Jonathan's problem about doing it himself.

However, Gretchen managed to convey nearly all the information I have given here in as small a space. She even added more specifics about the farm. What, then, is the advantage, if there is any, of my revision?

Is the acted-out opening more interesting? Does it catch your attention and focus it? Do you find yourself looking at Jonathan's problem through Jonathan's own eyes, wanting to see him escape from that endless row of corn? If you do, then the revision I have offered is working. The strength of modern fiction is that the reader participates in a story, not as an observer from the outside but from inside the main character. The story allows us to look out through that character's eyes, hear with his ears, think with his thoughts, feel with his feelings.

And that is what *show, don't tell* is all about.

You might like to take "The Air Pie" and revise it yourself. Work toward the same ending—that Jonathan is going to get his comeuppance for refusing to do "wommin's" work—but write the story again.

Move through the same three events: Jonathan's refusal to weed the corn, his getting his sister to collect the eggs for him, his resting under the tree while she picks blackberries. Use action and dialogue this time instead of summing up in a storyteller's voice. And when the ending comes, let us experience it with Jonathan. How does it feel to be offered an air pie when you were looking forward to succulent blackberries?

If you show instead of telling, you should find yourself with a stronger, more involving story.

Here is a very different kind of story by another young writer:

A Measly Five Dollars

Six gunshots are fired in the distance while Luke sits on his dirty, ripped couch searching once again for a vein to use. As he tightens the rubber tourniquet around his naked biceps, he thinks how much easier the drug will make it to pull this off. The cold needle pierces his weak skin; instantly he feels the hot liquid enter his veins. This is a trip he has taken many times before. His body begins to rush. His hands and legs tremble with adrenaline.

Luke reaches into the desk drawer and pulls out a loaded nine millimeter and places it between his belt and his sweaty skin. As he heads for the door, he picks up a smelly, wrinkled flannel shirt. Pulling it on, he quickens his pace down the stairs, making his way to the Jeep parked in front of the decaying housing development. He squeals away from the curb, his knuckles turning white as he grips the steering wheel with his drug-induced superhuman strength. Like a crazy man, he cruises through the city streets.

As Luke pulls into the old gas station on the out-skirts of L.A., his nervous energy is reaching its peak. He thinks of the drugs he will buy with the money he gets from this heist. He busts through the doors fero-ciously. Without thinking, Luke draws the gun from his belt. He aims it between the eyes of a young man behind the counter.

Luke starts to scream at the boy, but his voice is so loud, his voice can't be understood. The boy slowly, nervously reaches for the alarm button under the edge of the counter. But before the boy can press it, Luke quickly squeezes the trigger without regard for the young man's life. The bullet enters the boy, creating a gaping hole in his forehead.

As Luke moves around the counter to reach the cash, he steps on the lifeless body in a pool of blood. He forcefully hits the cash register with the butt of his gun. He rejoices as the till opens. What he sees in there is a disappointment at best.

A measly five dollars.

Jason Jaeger
Grade 8
Waseca Middle School
Waseca, Minnesota

This author moves in closer to the main character than Gretchen did in "The Air Pie." We feel the rush of the drugs, the intensity of Luke's purpose. Jason also has managed to make a strong point without moraliz-ing. When Luke opens the cash register to find "a measly five dollars," we know, without being told, that Luke's way is not one to follow.

However, though "A Measly Five Dollars" does use more direct action than the previous story, Jason still summarizes a great deal. As a reader, I don't respond to summaries. For instance, I feel very little when the clerk dies. Why? Because he hasn't become real to me. I haven't seen him. I haven't heard him speak. Luke hasn't reacted to him in any way. If he had, I would have had a chance to react, too.

Luke is not a main character we are expected to like. But if he sees the boy's terror and pain in close detail, I will see it, too. Then, despite Luke's indifference, my compassion will go out to the boy.

We begin the story inside Luke, feeling the tourniquet, the hot liquid in the vein, the trembling of his limbs, the gun tucked next to his sweaty skin. But as the story moves on, Jason moves further away from his main character. He tells us more and shows us less.

I see the gaping hole in the boy's forehead. It's the kind of detail that brings the moment to life, but I don't see it through Luke's eyes, and I no longer know what the world looks and feels like to Luke. What does he scream when he walks into the store that the boy can't understand? How does he know the clerk is reaching for an alarm button? What does he see when the boy falls? Is there some detail about the boy that would bring him to life for the reader even as Luke fails to respond to the boy's humanity?

While Jason has done a fine job of presenting a difficult subject, the story could be heightened considerably if he allowed more of the important details to be acted out. Doing so would require more length, of course, but that would be fine. As it stands, Jason's story is over before we have had a chance to feel its impact.

You might have a hard time working with this particular story. Luke is not the kind of character most of us can easily locate inside ourselves. The author himself probably found it difficult to get too close to such a person. That may be why he pulled back and began to summarize. But if you think you can imagine what the world might look like to a desperate drug addict, then you might try rewriting this story.

Imagine what it is like to be high. Consider Luke's desperate desire for more drugs. Climb inside his skin and let us know what he is thinking, feeling. Or, perhaps more appropriately in this story, consider what Luke is seeing but not reacting to as the rest of us would. What does the world look like when all normal feelings of human empathy are suppressed?

Feel the cool weight of the gun in Luke's hand. Stand across the counter from the terrified boy. Stare into the nearly empty cash register. Can you find words for what you discover? Can you play out this moment of the story?

Can you show us instead of telling us what happens here?

We all love being told a story. Living one is an even stronger experience. And part of the showing that makes it possible for readers to live your story is carefully detailed description. It can bring each character, each moment to satisfying life.

In the next chapter we will look at descriptive writing.

CHAPTER 3

Using the Senses . . . Description

Learning to write good fiction is a complex task made more difficult by the fact that it requires skills rarely used in other types of writing. When we write essays, reports, or even poems, we seldom use dialogue. *Show, don't tell* isn't a requirement for a good letter. And newspaper articles are not known for delving into their subjects' thoughts and feelings.

Descriptive writing is the exception, though. We use it in many kinds of writing besides fiction. Often, however, writers get so involved in mastering the new techniques demanded in producing a story that they forget what they know about descriptive writing. They even forget how much fun descriptive writing can be.

Here is a young author who hasn't forgotten. Take note of the description in this story.

No Harm Will Come to Good

The horses' hooves plop-plopped softly against the snow. The delicate little bells on their harness jingled merrily as they pranced down the road. They shivered as the winter air blew on their chestnut-brown coats. It was bitterly cold; perhaps it was below zero. It warmed one's spirit, though, to think about a blazing fire or a nice hot cup of chocolate.

The steady rhythm of the horses slowed as they approached McClugin's General Store. This was the only store that opened at 7:00 A.M. and closed at 4:00 P.M. Old Mr. McClugin didn't believe in keeping up with society. His store was the same way it had been twenty-some years ago when it first opened in 1839. The driver, Jacob McNaire, stepped down from his buggy and walked into the store.

It was quite dusty inside. Jacob McNaire immediately coughed. It almost seemed as if that made the old building shake. The fragile wooden counter looked as if it could fall apart at the slightest touch. Sitting on the counter was a display of cigar boxes that were at least three years old. Above the counter were shelves filled with dried foods. Hickory and cinnamon sticks were lying on the counter, along with other kinds of spices. Towards the end of the second counter was candy: sassafras, root beer, and peppermint sticks, all available at two for a penny. There were also newspapers neatly stacked next to the cracker barrel. In the back of the room, there was a large counter where Mr. McClugin sold fishing gear.

To the left of the counter sat Mr. McClugin himself, reading last week's newspaper. Just on the other side of the room there were barrels filled with molasses. In front of the barrels were huge sacks of coffee beans. The aroma was so rich and heavy one could smell it out on the street. There was a limited supply of cornmeal, which was kept in the back so no one could steal it.

Mr. McClugin also had what he liked to call the ladies' section, which was in the front. He regularly stocked things like needles, thread, and yarn. Hanging on three dingy nails were three lovely bonnets. One was yellow, one was blue, and the last was light pink. Mr. McClugin was quite proud of these delicate hats, for he had made them himself.

He also had a fine selection of buttons. His buttons ranged from beautiful white pearly to lovely lavender. There were some in a charming light blue and sky blue which were dainty and stylish, and gorgeous pinks that were simply delightful. The ladies seemed to be most fond of the enchanting hand-painted ones. Some had attractive English homes painted precisely on them. Others had tiny little flowers or portraits. Everyone seemed to fall in love with these fragile little buttons. The women also got excited over his fine selection of lace and ribbons. He also had a few rolls of cloth which were light blue and yellow.

Mr. McClugin went to the fireplace and put another piece of wood on the fire. He was a short man, the age of fifty with dark blue eyes and a sinister grin. He was not well educated, and he spoke English with a slight accent. A widower with little money, Mr. McClugin always appeared hunched over as if he were looking for his glasses on the ground. . . .

Anahid Thompson
Grade 5
Woodbury School
Shaker Heights, Ohio

And the story goes on from there. Jacob McNaire leaves the store thinking about shutting it down. In the end, though, after the store has been robbed and Mr. McClugin left bankrupt, Jacob decides to help the old man fix the place up.

Anahid uses description beautifully. We start out hearing the horses and the "delicate little bells on their harnesses," feeling the cold winter air. The inside of the store is described, both the details of what is sold there and the general sense of age and decay, in careful detail.

Even the characters are presented with images that make them come instantly to life, such as Mr. McClugin, who "always appeared hunched over as if he were looking for his glasses on the ground" and the fact that he, whose store is behind the times in every respect, is "reading last week's newspaper." Even his reading is behind the times!

There are moments, perhaps, when the description isn't quite consistent. For instance, in the first paragraph the hooves of the horses are first referred to as "plop-plopp[ing] softly against the snow," and in the next sentence the horses are said to have "pranced down the road." A plop-plopping sound would seem to refer to a walking horse, not a prancing one. Mr. McClugin is also said to have a "sinister grin," but nothing revealed about him seems sinister. In fact, the story shows him to be simply a very behind-the-times man who needs help.

But these are minor problems in what is otherwise rich and creative description. There is, however, another issue here entirely. The description overwhelms the story. In fact, we are well into "No Harm Will Come to Good," and we still don't know what the story problem is. The background for the story has been laid out, but the story itself hasn't yet begun.

Description needs to slide into a story like a snake through grass—silently, almost invisibly, without calling attention to itself. It should enrich every story moment without slowing the action. And action is what the early pages of this story lack. Anahid has concentrated so completely on description that she hasn't launched the action of the story at all.

Another point to consider: in contemporary stories description almost always comes through the perceptions of the characters, usually the main character. The author doesn't look down like God and describe the scene.

Imagine how much more we would learn about Jacob McNaire if we discovered the store and Mr. McClugin through his eyes. Imagine, too, how much more interested we would be in the store if the description were interwoven with action.

You might try to do both. Rewrite this opening so that we see the store through Jacob's eyes. Let him look around the place and think how out-of-date it is, how sorry he is to have his money tied up in such a pathetic business. Let him talk to Mr. McClugin, pointing out all that's wrong with the store. This should give the story more life. It should also move the action forward while still using some of the details from Anahid's fine description.

Here is another story that uses description well. In this one the author does an exceptionally good job of integrating description with story action.

The story is about a small angel named Holly who has been sent to earth on a Christmas mission, a mission which, if she is successful, will earn her her wings. I'll begin when the story is already under way.

31

Holly's Christmas Mission

. . . As she walked into a department store, Holly encountered a skinny man with scraggly whiskers dressed as Santa Claus.

"Hello, my child," he greeted in a scratchy voice. "Would you, by any chance, have a donation to give to the Salvation Army?"

"Why, I think I do, sir," replied Holly as she counted out her last bit of change.

"Thank you, sweetie," the man rejoiced.

Just then, a distinguished-looking gentleman wearing an expensive overcoat and a black top hat approached the store. Impulsively, Santa greeted him. "Merry Christmas, sir, isn't it a pretty day?"

Holly looked up to observe the encounter.

"Humph," snorted the well-dressed man, the creases on his forehead deepening. He had a salt-and-pepper goatee that was meticulously trimmed.

"Would you like to donate something to the Salvation Army? Your money would be going to a real good cause, of course," the sidewalk Santa reassured him, holding up the big black pot for donations.

"No," the grumpy man refused in a stern, harsh voice. His cloudy, gray eyes flared with anger.

"Yes, well, that's fine, too." Santa withdrew his slight figure. "Have a nice day, anyhow."

The rude man made no reply and disappeared into the crowd.

Holly looked up at the sad sidewalk Santa and smiled. "Here you are," she said, handing him a small, yet appreciated donation.

"Thank you so much, dearie."

"You're welcome. I'm just glad I could help," answered the angel. Her green eyes sparked with curiosity as she added, "Say, by any chance, do you know that man who just came by?"

The friendly Santa paused for a minute and looked up into the crisp Christmas air. "Why, yes, I do," he answered thoughtfully. "His name is George Humphrey. I don't know much about him besides the fact that he's a rich miser, if you excuse me for saying so."

Holly nodded anxiously, eager to learn more about Mr. Humphrey. In the back of her mind, she thought he could be part of her Christmas mission.

"Guess old man Humphrey just never learned himself how to love. Never was married. He's really loaded, but never gave one cent to those in need. Not one. Guess he just keeps all that money for himself, lets it build up in the bank. But that's all I know about Mr. Humphrey. That's all I know." Santa's blue eyes dropped back down to look directly at Holly. "That answer your question, dearie?"

Holly grinned widely. "Yes, sir, it does." She slowly pulled her hand out of her back pocket. "I don't suppose you know where Mr. Humphrey lives?"

The old man shook his head grimly. "No, I don't," he admitted.

"Well, I better be going," Holly said mischievously as she eyed the rest of the busy sidewalk. "But thank you very much, sir."

The skinny Santa proudly smiled, wrinkles appearing on his withered face. "Glad to oblige."

With the words "Merry Christmas," Holly dashed down the long avenue, hoping to catch a glimpse of George Humphrey.

She scurried down the long avenue as fast as her legs could carry her. "Oh," she cried out, pausing to catch her breath, "I just lost sight of him!"

She strained her eyes forward hoping desperately to spot him. Holly squealed in delight when she saw a black top hat similar to the one Mr. Humphrey was wearing come forth from the crowd. Gaining enthusiasm once more, she continued on her way.

Soon the hopeful angel approached the end of the avenue in which there was a four-way intersection. Holly lifted her eyes off the top hat for just a moment to observe the traffic, but it was a long-enough break to lose sight of her suspect.

With disappointment, the girl chose no particular street and trudged along. As Holly's walk proceeded she found herself getting into a gloomier, less-crowded boulevard. She looked up toward the sky and found snow-covered trees guarding the unfamiliar path. "Oh, God," she murmured soberly, "please help me find Mr. Humphrey. Please." Becoming but a whisper, her feeble voice trailed off into the silence.

At the sound of wind whistling through the barren trees, Holly felt a tingle run down her spine. She looked out to her right and there, in the middle of what seemed to be nowhere, was an old mansion.

Building up all her courage, the timid angel opened the gate of a tall, black wrought-iron fence. As a loud screech pierced the air, Holly shuddered uncomfortably. Forcing herself to persevere, walking along the weed-covered path, she felt her palms gather sweat. Holly walked up the steps with reluctance. Standing right in front of the door, she read the engraving on the large, lion's head knocker. Squinting to see through the rust, Holly sharply drew in her breath and read . . . George M. Humphrey.

Squeezing her eyes shut with fright, Holly firmly gripped the brass knocker and gave it two hard pounds. She waited a minute then repeated her action.

Finally the door opened, and two cloudy gray eyes instantly jumped on her, as a predator approaching its prey would.

Backing off, Holly stuttered awkwardly, "H-h-hello, Mr. Humphrey."

"Who are you?" Mr. Humphrey demanded in a stern, rough voice. He stayed hidden behind the big door.

"Me?" Holly questioned shyly, pointing to her chest.

The miser narrowed his eyes and barked, "Yes, you. Who else?"

"Well, I'm Holly, sir." She smiled gently and looked closely into his eyes. "I saw you at the department store, remember?"

The grumpy man frowned and paused for a minute. "If you've come for money," he replied in a harsh voice, "the answer's no."

The angel giggled hoarsely. "No, sir, I haven't come for money. I just wanted to pay you a visit. No particular reason."

Mr. Humphrey remained standing there in the same exact position, hands on hips and face all crunched up.

Holly sensed that her answer was not enough for him, so she added softly, "I hoped we could be friends, Mr. Humphrey. That's all."

The old man nodded sourly and eyed Holly. "Fine. You may come in."

35

She silently rejoiced and entered the old mansion.

Mr. Humphrey stiffly led the way through a long, dreary hallway. Though the once-fine maroon carpet was faded and stained, it was marvelously woven. Classical paintings hung on the walls, accumulating dust. Holly could tell the mansion had once been filled with modern riches.

Still without comment, Mr. Humphrey stalked into a spacious room. Aside from a few big chairs, an end table and a beautifully carved coffee table, the room was empty.

"Sit down," ordered Mr. Humphrey, studying the frightened, yet excited angel like a hawk.

She nodded eagerly and plopped down onto a worn, old-fashioned chair. "Thank you, Mr. Humphrey. Thank you very much."

The old man acknowledged Holly's gratitude with but a tilt of his head. He sat down uneasily.

"Like I said earlier, Mr. Humphrey," Holly said lightly, "I came here to get to know you."

The miser squinted his eyes as the creases on his face doubled. Drawing up his finger, he slowly rubbed his goatee.

The smart girl realized now she perhaps would need to stretch the truth a bit to accomplish her goal. "I've heard you're a nice gentleman," she hinted.

[The story is too long to reproduce here in its entirety. I will tell you, though, that through a few rather unangelic maneuvers that involve giving Mr. Humphrey reason to believe, suddenly, that he is poor, Holly is successful in her mission. Now let's skip to the story's closing paragraph.]

Walking out of the bank with a newfound spring in his step, George headed toward the post office.

Unknown to Mr. Humphrey, the check he was mailing was the largest single donation ever received by the very appreciative Children's Fund.

Rounding the corner of the town's department store, George spotted the same sidewalk Santa ringing the Salvation Army bell. This time, however, George emptied his pockets into the big black pot.

At that exact moment, Holly completed her Christmas mission and earned her wings.

Christina Capecchi
Grade 6
Convent of the Visitation School
Mendota Heights, Minnesota

Notice what a fine job Christina has done weaving the description throughout her story. We see the skinny Santa as Holly sees him . . . and go on seeing him as the two talk. We see Mr. Humphrey when he enters the store, too, his expensive overcoat and black top hat, his salt-and-pepper goatee that is meticulously trimmed, the way his forehead creases when the Salvation Army Santa greets him.

Instead of the narrator's giving us background information about Mr. Humphrey, Holly gets it from the Santa through dialogue. And when she follows Mr. Humphrey to his home, the author doesn't stop the story to describe his house. We see each aspect as Holly discovers the place, from the "wind whistling through the barren trees" to the rusty lion's head knocker to the "once-fine maroon carpet . . . faded and stained" but "marvelously woven."

We encounter Mr. Humphrey with Holly, seeing with her eyes, hearing with her ears. He speaks in a stern, rough voice, nods sourly, squints his eyes. Christina gives us a complex experience of this character without ever pausing in the forward movement of her story to "describe." The story keeps flowing. That doesn't mean a writer should never pause for a paragraph of description, but description interwoven with a forward-moving story is usually the most effective.

As often happens when good writers are first learning to use descriptive language, some of Christina's descriptions are a bit heavy, especially in her use of adverbs. A few of the -*ly* words Christina uses are effective. Most could be eliminated without loss. Christina also has a tendency to repeat certain sentence patterns too close together, especially participial phrases such as "Standing right in front of the door . . ." However, her overall description is not only vivid but a natural part of her story.

Good description in stories involves more than pausing now and then to take note of the weather or the color of a character's eyes. Good description takes into account important action, playing it out so that it comes to life. Go back and reread the scene when Holly approaches Mr. Humphrey's house. If a moment is dramatically important, it needs to be played out through the senses and through the main character's thoughts and feelings as Christina has done here.

When you tell a story, don't forget to weave descriptions into it. Your story world will come to life if you make use of your main character's senses. And the story action, interwoven with description, will be exciting and real.

Now let's look at a less familiar writing technique, but one that is essential in stories . . . dialogue.

CHAPTER 4

The Art of Conversation... Dialogue

Dialogue in stories serves many functions. It gives the reader information. It reveals character. It moves the story forward. And it does all this while keeping the story active and breaking up the print on the page to make reading more inviting.

Many beginning writers have a hard time with dialogue, however. Either they tend to forget to use it at all or they try to tell an entire story through conversation. Let's begin by examining a story that could be made stronger by introducing more dialogue.

The Legend of Vampire Valley

The warm summer sun was setting behind the high hill. Darkness began to blanket the land. A small boy stepped out of the shadows. He felt something cold and damp nudge his leg. The boy swerved around and, spotting his dog, said, "What are you doing here, girl? No dogs are supposed to be out at night, and you know that. You could have been killed by one of the vampires. Why are you following me around in the dead of night?"

The dog didn't answer. Instead, she started howling.

The boy began to wonder what his dog was doing. He turned his attention toward the hill. There, a man dressed in black appeared over the horizon. The boy jumped back in surprise when the man threw his cape violently over his shoulders. Immediately, the man's clothes fell to the ground. The boy was scared because the man was no longer there.

He could hear his heart thumping. He wondered if it would burst out of his chest. The boy walked ever so cautiously toward the pile of clothes and poked at them, expecting a monster or some other hideous creature to appear. Nothing happened. The boy, feeling more confident, grabbed the clothes and flung them into the air.

Suddenly bats, thousands of bats, filled the night sky. The boy, shocked with terror, was rooted to the ground. He heard his dog howling painfully. They had her!

The boy felt a sudden gust of wind blowing through the air. It released him from the invisible cage. The boy seized his chance to escape and raced down the hill. He could feel the air rushing by. The bats were in hot pursuit.

Suddenly the bats stopped chasing him. Instead, they flapped their wings rapidly and floated in the air. The boy stopped running and caught his breath. He watched the bats as they gradually melted together into a thick black mob. The boy tried to make out what they were melting into.

A vampire! The boy suddenly realized that the bats

had formed a vampire with fangs and claws. The boy's eyes opened wide with horror, and he found himself gasping for breath. He screamed and ran toward town, but all the people had vanished into thin air.

He was the only one left.

The vampire flew into the air and swooped low over his head, forcing the boy to trip. The boy tried to scramble to his feet, but the ground began trembling. Soon the earth opened its jaws and swallowed the boy, along with the remainder of his town. Now, all that's left is a valley, a Valley of Vampires.

Jennifer Lee
Grade 5
Ridgewood Elementary School
Renton, Washington

"The Legend of Vampire Valley" has a great deal of exciting action, well played out. Jennifer does a particularly good job of letting us feel the horror of the moment through sharing the boy's physical reactions. When she tells us, "The boy was scared," we feel little. But when she says, "He could hear his heart thumping. He wondered if it would burst out of his chest," we are drawn into his terror.

This story, however, has little dialogue. There is, of course, an obvious reason for its having so little. With the exception of the dog, present only in the opening, there is no one in the scene for the main character to talk to.

Let's begin, though, by considering what the boy says to the dog as the story opens. Notice, first, how urgent the situation feels when he is talking. Much more urgent than it seems later when the narrator is simply telling us what is going on. What we are missing here, however, is any kind of a response from the dog. We have a monologue, not dialogue.

Now I assume that Jennifer doesn't intend "The Legend of Vampire Valley" to be the kind of story in which dogs talk. But take a look at this small revision I have made that allows the dog some perfectly doglike responses:

The boy swerved around and, spotting his dog, said, "What are you doing here, girl?"

The dog made no response, just cocked her head and gazed at her master intently.

"No dogs are supposed to be out at night, and you know that. You could have been killed by one of the vampires."

The dog still sat there. Except for her eyes, alert, intent on her master's face, she might have been made out of stone. When the boy turned to move away, though, she moved with him, staying as close to his heels as his own shadow.

The boy whirled, speaking more sharply this time. "Why are you following me around in the dead of night?"

The dog didn't answer. Instead, she started howling.

Note how breaking up the dialogue and including the dog's responses—even though they are not articulate responses—brings the reader into the scene more sharply. By focusing on the dog during the breaks in the dialogue, the writer also gives the reader a stronger feeling for her so that later, when she is taken by the bats, the loss will matter more.

There are two ways in which dialogue could be employed in the rest of the story. Jennifer could have the boy talking to himself, or she could provide an opportunity for conversation by introducing another character.

Many beginning writers attempt to create stories involving only one character, as Jennifer has done here. While not an impossible task, it is a difficult one. It is difficult precisely because, without dialogue, stories usually lack intimacy. And if readers don't feel an intimate connection with the main character, they won't feel even the strongest action as much as they should.

Because "The Legend of Vampire Valley" is complete in so few words, this would be a good story to use as a frame for practicing writing dialogue. Either you could create another character who encounters the vampires with the boy, or you could have the boy talk in short bursts, even though no one is there to respond.

Here is another story, untitled, that makes good use of dialogue:

Ty was very excited about going to his new school. His first class was gym, and that was his favorite. When Ty got there, all the other kids were outside. "Go ahead and get dressed," said the teacher.

"Okay, what are we playing?" asked Ty.

"Kickball," said Mr. Dukes.

"Cool, I'll be right out," Ty said excitedly.

Ty hurried and got dressed and ran outside as fast as he could. When he got to the field, all the kids were in line to get picked for teams.

"We want Ben," said the blue team's captain.

"We'll take Joe," said the captain of the red team.

Adam, the captain of the blue team, said, "We'll take Shelly."

Stacy, the red team's captain, said, "We want Molly."

The two teams went on picking the kids, and soon Ty was the only one who hadn't been picked. All the kids went running to the field, and Ty stood by the sidewalk all alone. Mr. Dukes came over and said, "Ty, why don't you go out with the blue team. You can pitch."

"Okay," Ty said with a shaky voice.

"First kicker!" yelled Mr. Dukes.

No one moved. They all just sat there and stared at Ty.

"First kicker!" yelled Mr. Dukes, twice as loud as before.

Joe went up to the plate. "Roll the ball, black boy," said Joe.

Ty just stood there.

"Are you deaf, nigger?" said Joe.

Ty ran off the field. The rest of the day he was very sad because all day the kids continually teased him, especially Joe Macintosh. When the time finally came for Ty's mom to pick him up from school, he was so upset that the first thing he said was, "I'm never going back there."

"What's wrong, Tyrone?" asked his mother.

"The kids at school hate me."

"You're just new. You'll make friends soon. Just have patience."

"You don't understand, Mom. They don't like me because I'm black."

"Oh, Ty, you're being silly. There are plenty of black kids at school."

"No, Mom. I'm the only one."

"Ty, you make it sound like a disease."

"Sometimes it feels like it. They all stare and call you names like nigger. Boy, I hate that word."

"Who called you that?"

"Joe Macintosh, mostly."

"Well, I'm going to have to call his mom. Kids shouldn't say such vulgar things. What did you say his last name was?"

"Macintosh. His dad owns the hardware store downtown."

"555-1001."

"Hello. Harry's Hardware. Mr. Macintosh speaking."

"Mr. Macintosh, this is Mrs. Jackson. We just moved here, and it seems that your son Joe is making it very hard for my son, Ty, to fit in."

"Well, Joseph has told me all about your son, and the whole town is talking about you. I already know what I need to."

"You don't quite understand. He called Ty a nigger."

"Well, that's what he is, isn't he?"

"Excuse me. What did you say?"

"I don't care to discuss this with you. Goodbye."

The next day at school things only got worse. Ty's locker was all messed up with nigger written in big bold red letters on the door. Ty immediately went to the principal, but no one confessed to seeing anyone around his locker. After lunch, a crowd of boys, including Joe, confronted Ty.

"My dad said your mom called him yesterday," said Joe.

"Yes, so?"

"So now I'm gonna have to teach you a lesson. I'll see you after school."

Sure enough, right after school Joe and his gang were waiting for Ty. Ty tried to avoid walking by them, but Joe quickly caught up.

"What's wrong? Are you chicken?" said Joe.

"I have no reason to fight you, Joe," stated Ty.

"Well, I have a reason to fight you."

Before Ty had time to reply, Joe had him on the ground. All the kids were cheering for Joe.

Just as Joe raised his fist, Mr. Shank, the history teacher, broke up the fight. "Will someone please tell me what's going on?"

"He started it," replied Joe.

"Did not," said Ty.

"Well, I'm sure the principal will get to the bottom of this. Come on, boys. Let's go. Principal Jones, these two were fighting across the street."

"Thanks, Mr. Shank. Okay, boys, what's going on? Why are you two fighting?"

"I didn't want to, sir. He started the whole thing," stated Ty.

"No, he started it by getting me in trouble," said Joe.

"Well, since you two can't seem to get along, I'm going to see you both after school for the next week, or until you learn to get along. I'll call your parents and tell them you'll be staying with me for an hour each day starting today. In the meantime, get your gym clothes on and help me with my free throws. I know you like basketball, Joe. What about you, Ty?"

"Yes, I love to play. I was the starting point guard at my old school."

"Well, good. See, you two already have something in common." . . .

Tina Overmyer
Grade 11
North Baltimore High School
North Baltimore, Ohio

I will stop the story there, though you can already get a glimpse of the way in which the story's resolution will come about. Tina's dialogue has an authentic sound, like real people talking. She does a good job of revealing the story problem through what people say, too. However, as can easily happen, once the author gets started with dialogue, she seems to have a hard time moving back into her narration. The dialogue takes over. We don't see Ty and his mother get home, don't see his mother pick up the phone, we just hear her recite the number she is dialing. This is awkward.

Another problem here is that the dialogue stands alone too much of the time. We should be looking at the world from Ty's point of view, seeing, hearing, thinking, feeling with him. So when someone speaks to Ty, we should see that speaker through Ty's eyes. What is the person doing? What does he sound like?

For instance, when Joe walks up to the plate, what does he look like? What posture does he assume as he takes his place? When he says, "Roll the ball, black boy," does he smirk and look over his shoulder to see if he has his friends' support? Or does he glare at Ty defiantly? What is Ty thinking and feeling as he faces Joe?

Dialogue is powerful and important, but only in a play script can it stand alone. And there it needs no supporting narration because the actors, stage sets, and costumes will fill in all that surrounds the words . . . the

47

characters' appearance, the manner in which they speak, the place where the conversation occurs. When you are writing fiction, you must fill in those details as you go along. Not every possible detail, but enough to make the story come alive.

A useful exercise would be to return to any section of dialogue in Tina's story and write it again. Use the same dialogue, but this time include descriptions, through Ty's perceptions, of the speakers and the setting. Let us share Ty's thoughts and feelings, too. As discussed earlier, try not to put the description in long chunks. Slip it into and around the conversation.

And now a final example of a young writer's use of dialogue:

The Puppy Rescue

"He's so adorable!" twelve-year-old Sarah Dominion exclaimed, doing a double take as her brown ponytail swished around her head. She had not seen the little light-brown dog before, but when he put out his paw for a shake, she gladly accepted and shook the paw.

Sarah was at the shelter once again as she always was after school, doing volunteer work. She had gone to the Animal Shelter ever since her class had a bake sale to raise money for the filled shelter.

Her aunt Elisabeth, the kennel master, was cleaning out a cage across the room, so Sarah asked, "What's going to happen to this puppy over here?"

Aunt Elisabeth looked over at her and the dog. "Well, he's part of the sick bunch, so unfortunately the doctor said we should put him to sleep if he's not picked up by next week."

"Oh . . . ," Sarah said, a little angrily.

Sarah's mom, Amanda, was Aunt Elisabeth's older sister, so she knew that her aunt was really depressed about putting the little puppy to sleep. But she was still angry that anyone would do that to an animal.

"No, you can't do that!" she said in a high-pitched voice, all the while trying not to cry. "Not to Honey!" She didn't know why she was crying, but she couldn't help it. She was never that emotional.

"Honey?" Elisabeth questioned.

"Well . . . that's what I named him," she said, embarrassed. She didn't know why she had said it, but it did fit him quite well.

"Sarah, you know that happens to all the animals here who don't get adopted. I'm sorry, but you can't get too attached."

"But he hasn't even begun to grow!" Immediately she was sorry. Aunt Elisabeth knew how it felt to get attached, because about a year ago she had gotten attached to a dog named Chocolate who had died of cancer. "I'm sorry, Aunt Elisabeth. I know you can't help it."

"I'm sorry, too, Sarah," she said with tears in her eyes. "Look, I'll talk to you tonight, but right now I have to go to the board meeting. I'll see you later."

"Okay. Have a good meeting," Sarah whispered, feeling very depressed. . . .

Annemarie Ziegler
Grade 6
Trinity Catholic School
Tallahassee, Florida

Notice how much information Annemarie has wound in and around her dialogue. We get a quick summation of the situation—where Sarah is and why she is there—but more important, we get Sarah's feelings and some sense of who Aunt Elisabeth is. What is said is important, but the information woven around the conversation is equally so. We hear Sarah's voice rise as she becomes more and more emotional over the puppy. We see the tears in Aunt Elisabeth's eyes. We even sense that Sarah is violating the rules by getting so attached when Aunt Elisabeth questions, rather starkly, "Honey?" And all the way through, we know what Sarah is feeling.

The author could use Sarah's senses more, let us see the puppy in more detail, feel his paw in Sarah's hand, hear an edge in Aunt Elisabeth's voice or see an expression flit across her face. She has, however, been very successful with what she has given us.

The first principle of dialogue is that the people talking must sound like real people talking. But beyond the words that are said, the author has an opportunity to weave in all sorts of riches: sensory impressions, feelings, plans for what the main character intends to do next.

Try it. The weaving can be fun.

Next let's consider the most important single aspect of any piece of fiction . . . character.

CHAPTER 5

Character...the Heart of Fiction

Good stories are written every day. Some of these stories are even published. But only a small proportion of these good stories survive to be read and passed on to new generations. The main reason some do survive is that their authors have succeeded in making the characters seem like real people.

Bringing characters to life is the most interesting and the most difficult task facing any writer.

Think about the characters in this next story.

Emergency!

A siren sounded! Workers ran! Lights flashed! Is it happening, or is it a drill? The owner, Ur Ainium Tothirtyfive, was standing there, quietly timing them. When the building was evacuated, he stopped his stopwatch. "Seven minutes, thirty-five seconds!" he shouted. "In a real nuclear meltdown, this place would be up in flames in five minutes flat! We need to work on this, people!"

A young worker, Plu Tonium was his name, walked up to the tall, broad-chested man of forty-five. "Boss," he said, inquiring, "why are we always running these stupid drills? It's not like there's ever actually going to *be* a meltdown. We're safe workers. You should teach us to *prevent* a meltdown, not evacuate when there *is* a meltdown!"

"Kid," U.T. started, "we could be fully automated with no problems and still have a meltdown. We *do* need to practice!" And with that, he stalked angrily to his office.

"Over-the-hill people," the worker thought. "You know I hate 'em." He returned to his messy workstation and resumed his work.

A week later, there was another meltdown drill. They scored six minutes, twenty seconds. A good time, comparatively.

"I'm impressed, people! You're doing better!" Ur yelled, happiness in his voice. He strode to his office, smiling.

There were drills twice a week after that. Times were as low as four minutes, seventeen seconds. Ur Ainium was always happy on drill days, and the work was prosperous.

One day Ur's secretary, Linda Schwartz, an unmarried lady of twenty-nine, received a telephone call. "Is Mr. Tothirtyfive in?" the caller wondered.

"He's in a meeting right now. May I take a message?" Linda replied, unaware of any impending danger.

"Turn the fax machine on. I'm going to fax something to you. Give the fax to your boss, and *don't* look at it!" Then the mysterious caller hung up.

Suddenly, the fax machine whirred to life. On its fax tray there lay a memo, made from newspaper and magazine clippings. It read: "Shut down the power plant by 5:30 tonight or I'll remove the control rods to melt down the plant!"

Linda ran nervously over to her desk and hit her intercom button. Ur answered. "Mr. Tothirtyfive! Come into my office! Quick!" Ms. Schwartz said, panting with every breath.

Ur came in, and Linda showed him the bizarre letter. He gasped. He looked at the clock . . . 4:30 P.M. He jumped over to his desk and hit the Meltdown Alarm. You could hear loud groans. Someone shouted, "Come on, boss. It's getting old!"

Ur hit the intercom. "This is *not* a drill!" Ur said. "There has been a threat to the plant. Evacuate yourselves and your belongings. The meltdown is at five-thirty. Move it, people. Move it!"

Within thirty seconds everyone was moving. Boxes were stacked at workstations. Everything was in chaos. Twenty-five minutes later, everyone was out of the building. Everyone except Ur Ainium Tothirtyfive. There was time still to stop the meltdown. And he was going to do it.

He carefully and slowly switched the control rods and the fuel rods. Then he hid in a dark corner and waited while hot beads of burning sweat dropped from his aching forehead. He looked neurotically at his gold-faced digital Timex watch. He pressed the IndiGLO button. The brightly lit display said 5:27. Three minutes left. It was so dead quiet, he could hear his own heart monotonously beating. Two minutes passed. 5:29. Just sixty seconds longer. Sixty heart-pounding seconds.

A tall, dark figure walked up to the control station. Ur estimated that whoever it was, he was twenty-two or twenty-three. The man hit a few controls. Ur could hear the control rods lifting out. He quietly scurried to a security panel and pressed the red lit 911 button.

Two minutes later, the cops arrived. They roped off the building and searched it. Hiding in the same corner that Ur Ainium Tothirtyfive had hidden in, they found Plu Tonium, the kid against the meltdown drills.

The policeman bent down to pick him up, and to their surprise their hands passed right through his now-translucent body. They looked around and saw a holographic projector.

They followed the cable on the projector around a corner and out a back door. On a small muddy piece of land, they saw a holographic recorder. The ground in front of the recorder was trampled from someone sitting there. There were large footprints leading away from the recorder. The police followed them cautiously and came to a trap door. They slowly opened the door to find Plu Tonium. He was on the floor, unmoving, unconscious. He had been hit over the head by someone.

A guilt-ridden figure ran out from the shadows. "Stop!" the lieutenant yelled, startled. The figure kept running, determined to outrun the now-chasing officers. He ran around a corner. There was a loud "thud." The police came to the dark passage and found a sheer, flat moldy wall. The figure lying on the floor was Ur Ainium Tothirtyfive. He, too, was now unconscious.

Two hours later in the emergency ward of Mercy Hospital . . . "Beep, beep, beep, beep, beeeeeeeeeep," the electrocardiogram was beeping one long monotonous beep. This particular EKG was hooked up to a patient named Ur Ainium Tothirtyfive. Standing over him was an unmasked doctor. He had just pulled out

Ur Ainium's IV's and put in 1,000 cc's (enough to kill) of thorazine (a high-power tranquilizer). The doctor left, Ur Ainium being dead.

Five minutes later, massive amounts of doctors, surgeons, and nurses piled into his room. They got the electrocardiostimulators (those things that bring you back to life), charged them up, and zapped him. There was a brief heartbeat, but it stopped. They zapped again. He slowly regained life.

Later, there was no sign of the murderous doctor. And no sign of Plu Tonium.

Jamey Hamilton
Grade 6
Neff School
Miamisburg, Ohio

"Emergency!" is well written. There is a good balance between dialogue and narration. Jamey is particularly adept at building tension. Go back and reread the two paragraphs that begin with "He carefully and slowly switched the control rods and the fuel rods." Notice the way in which we follow Ur Ainium's tension through every moment so that we, too, are feeling tense. And there is much high and important action. Yet, when Ur Ainium dies and then is brought back to life at the end, I felt nothing. What about you?

Why don't we feel Ur Ainium's peril . . . or the peril of the community when the nuclear plant is under threat, for that matter? Because none of the characters comes to life. We don't know who they are, why they are behaving as they do, or what they want.

Jamey probably didn't set out intending to create lifelike characters. If he had, he wouldn't have chosen names that represent elements rather than human

55

beings. And this is a choice he has a right to make. In making it, however, he sacrificed much of his readers' connection with "Emergency!"

We care about stories because we care about human beings—how they think, what they feel, whether they succeed or fail. When a writer chooses to give us a story without humans (or without stand-ins for humans, as we usually have with animal characters or science fiction creatures), the story must be extremely clever to hold our interest at all.

We never know why Plu Tonium objects so strongly to the drills. We have even less information about why he would hate his boss so much that he would attempt to kill him, except that he thinks Ur Ainium is "over the hill," which hardly seems enough. If Jamey were to decide to rewrite this story, developing his characters more fully, those would be the first questions he would need to answer.

He would need to know more about Ur, too. Is there something about him, beyond his obsession with getting the evacuation drills right, that might make someone want to murder him? Think through these questions and see if you can come up with answers that would involve us with these characters, make us care about them.

Here is a piece in which characters are more closely observed.

A Walk in the Park

I sat in the park and watched the young girl who sat in the park and watched the old man who sat in the park and stared at nothing. We were an interesting trio, the three of us. Me with my Armani suit, fifty-dollar tie, and Italian leather briefcase. The young girl, who could not be more than eight or nine, with her scabby knees and her lollipop grasped in her sticky hands. And the old man in his khakis and his cardigan, looking as if he had no idea where he was . . . or who.

And it was then it dawned on me. It dawned on me that I didn't know who he was. That there were millions of people in the world, billions! And I didn't know any of them. It dawned on me that these two, the girl with her frazzled pigtails and the old man with his too-thick, old-fashioned glasses, were going to leave this park soon and go home to lives which I could not even begin to imagine! No one in the world knew what it was like for ANYONE!

The little girl was getting bored; the man was no longer interesting. She put her lollipop in her mouth and buried her sandaled feet in the soft, brown sand. She picked up a handful of this childhood fairy dust and sprinkled it over her feet, burying them up to the ankle. She switched her gaze back to the old man, checking to see if he had become interesting in the past thirty seconds.

As she did this, the man pulled a hand from his pocket. Each movement of each muscle looked as if it pained him. He held in his hand a beautiful old pocket watch, obviously gold. (The girl's eyes widened, and she licked hungrily at the syrup on her fingers and lips.) The man stared vacantly at the watch in his hands, and I could pick out his thoughts like nuts from a bowl: "Where did this come from?"

The girl rose to her feet and dusted off her legs, getting the sand stuck to her saccharine fingers. She stared at her fingers for a minute, shook her head and smiled. She waved a hand in the direction of the old man. He smiled sweetly in return and turned to leave as the girl hopped on a cherry-red bicycle and rode off.

I stayed a moment after they'd left, watching the other children swing and play in the park. I then leaned over and picked up my Italian briefcase, sighed, and headed for home.

Jenna Carlson
Grade 10
St. Paul Academy and Summit School
Minneapolis, Minnesota

What Jenna has offered here is a character study, not a story. For it to be a story there would need to be some struggle, some change, at the very least a climactic moment of understanding. As this piece stands now, nothing happens. The observer notes in the beginning that it is impossible to know any other human being, and that observation proves to be true. We don't come to know any of these figures, including the observer.

The author has created some well-drawn moments, though, the kind that could be powerful in a story. The details of the way the girl watches the old man are finely observed. Growing bored, she turns her attention to her lollipop and to the soft brown sand beneath her feet. Then she checks again to see if the man "had become interesting in the past thirty seconds." I especially liked Jenna's phrase "I could pick out his thoughts like nuts from a bowl."

Within a story, character is relevant only as it relates to the story action. We don't want to know all the details of where a character was born and what he has for breakfast unless those facts reveal something about his relationship to the story problem. What we do seek to understand, always, are the motives behind every character's actions. Why does the main character want what she does? What (or who) is preventing her from getting what she wants? Why are others helping or hindering her in the course of her struggle?

Writing character sketches is an excellent way of teaching yourself to observe human beings. It is fine practice in probing the deep questions surrounding characters and their motivations. But the point of any story, even a story which sets out to prove that we know nothing about other human beings, is to penetrate at least one character. And Jenna's character sketch doesn't go on to do that.

By the end, we know nothing about the narrator beyond what we are given in the opening lines, the "Armani suit, fifty-dollar tie, and Italian leather briefcase." These are interestingly chosen externals, but readers want to find out more about the characters in stories, especially the perceiving character. One of the reasons we read stories is to break down our own sense of isolation by moving inside another thinking, feeling being. And stories that don't give us this intimate experience usually disappoint us.

Read this story next and note what the author does with characterization.

Forgiveness

"Doctor Butler, Doctor Butler, please report to room 209," came an announcement booming over the hospital's P.A. system.

I had been sitting in the hospital waiting room for what seemed like days. I looked at my watch. Seven hours. I had sent my mom home three hours ago because she was exhausted.

"I don't know, Jeff. I feel like I should stay here in case your father wakes up," she had said.

"Don't worry, Mom. If he does, I'll call. Now, go home and get some sleep."

"All right, hon. You promise to call?" she asked, her voice etched with concern.

"I promise, Mom," I said, forcing a smile that I didn't feel.

Her words echoed clearly in my mind. "In case your father wakes up." I replayed those words over again, asking myself what I would do if my father did wake up. I heard hushed whispers coming from across the room, and I looked up to see who it was. It was a young soldier comforting a crying girl. Taking a closer look at his uniform, I could see that he was assigned to a Special Forces unit. He was young, only a sergeant, in fact, but he looked at least a hundred years old.

"Man, imagine how you must look," I said to myself.

"Don't worry, sis. Mom will be okay," the young soldier said to the crying girl.

I found myself thinking back to my relationship with my father. It had deteriorated after I joined the army at the age of twenty-two. My father was a successful lawyer and wanted me to follow in his footsteps. I planned on doing so, but changed my mind right after getting accepted into the law school at Harvard University. I decided that I wanted to kill terrorists, so I took my degree in English and became an Infantry officer. My father was very displeased with my decision and felt that I had stabbed him in the back. We had not kept in touch since.

Things in my life had gone downhill since joining

the Army. My fiancée, deciding that marriage wasn't what she wanted after all, left me a week before we were scheduled to get married. Unable to cope with the pain or the empty feeling, I threw myself into work.

I was deployed to the Persian Gulf with my Delta Force team during Operation Desert Storm. We were given a mission to go in and rescue some U.S. P.O.W.'s. On this mission my best friend had made the ultimate sacrifice for me. A haunting image of his smiling face took me back to that night.

Sitting outside an Iraqi regimental headquarters building where our guys were supposedly being held, we looked at each other, reading the other's thoughts.

"Hey, Jeff, fifty bucks says I have to cover your butt on this operation," came the sound of his voice, cutting through the cold, desert air.

"No way, Sam. I'm the one covering for you all the time."

Suddenly gunfire erupted from everywhere, taking half the team out. "Ambush!" someone yelled.

"Move it, Jeff!" Sam yelled, snapping me out of my state of shock. We ran for the east fence where we had infiltrated into the camp. Out of nowhere a figure popped up out of the sand, his rifle aimed right at my chest. Petrified, I stood there, unable to move. Sam pushed me out of the way as the Iraqi pulled the trigger on his rifle. I saw Sam's body gyrate with the force of the bullets striking him. My instincts took over and I grabbed my rifle, sending a bullet into the Iraqi's face. His head erupted into a geyser of gray matter and red mist. I ran over to Sam's body, taking him in my arms. He looked up at me, his eyes still smiling. "I guess you owe me fifty bucks, huh?"

"Yeah, I guess I do, buddy," I said, feeling his life escape as his blood seeped through my fingers. Staining the ground with the innocence of a man who had no place in this war, a man who should have been at home with his wife and two kids, not dying in this godforsaken desert.

After the mission I retreated into myself and shut out everyone I cared about, including my parents. I was later awarded a Distinguished Service Cross for valor. I never felt that I had earned it. I had taken it to Sam's grave and left it there, feeling it was the only way I could thank him. My father had received a letter from the Army telling him about the award I received in the Gulf.

"Jeff," I heard my dad's voice, distant over the phone.

"Hi, Dad."

"You could have let us know that you were given such a high award for valor. You should have at least called us. We never heard a thing from you. Your mom has been worried sick."

"Dad, since when have you cared about my military career? You shut me out when I decided to join the Army. You're to blame for the years of silence. I haven't needed you so far, and I don't need you now!" I yelled into the phone, feeling some of the bottled-up hurt from all the years of silence come gushing out.

"What's your problem, young man?"

"You! So just leave me alone!" I yelled into the phone, then slammed it down.

My father and I had not spoken since that day.

Then I received the call from my mom. My father had passed out and had been rushed to the hospital.

He had slipped into a coma. I had debated whether or not even to come to the hospital, thinking my father wouldn't even want me to be there. I told my mother as much.

"No, Jeff, you have to," she'd pleaded with me. "I need you here."

My thoughts were interrupted by a hand on my shoulder. Startled, I looked up into the face of an unfamiliar doctor. His name tag read Dr. Jacobs.

"Hey there, Jeff. How you doing?" he asked with sincere concern.

"Not too well," I told him, puzzled by his knowing my name.

He seemed to read my mind. "I'm a specialist. They called me in to look at your father. You look like you could use some help, too. Want to talk about it?"

"Well," I said, hesitating. Could I pour my heart out to a stranger? Somehow he seemed different, like he actually cared. I decided to tell him.

Tears of frustration spilled out of my eyes. "I just wish I could tell him that I love him before he dies."

"Why don't you go in and see him," he said, as if he knew something I didn't.

"All right. One second. Let me grab my stuff," I said, turning around. When I stood up he was gone.

Suddenly a sense of urgency filled me. I ran down the hall to my father's room. I burst in, stopping by his bed.

"Please, wake up, if only for a minute. I've got to tell you something," I whispered, taking his hand.

Suddenly I felt his hand move. I saw his eyes opening.

"Dad," I whispered.

"Jeff, is that you?" came a faint reply.

"I've got something to tell you."

"Don't worry, son. I forgive you. It's over."

"No, Dad. I have to tell you something."

"Don't worry. I know," he said, closing his eyes and smiling. I could feel his grip on my hand weakening.

"I love you, Dad," I whispered, feeling his life escape.

I slowly released his hand and walked out into the hall. Stopping a passing nurse, I asked her if she knew where I could find Dr. Jacobs.

She gave me a quizzical look. "Who?" she asked.

"Dr. Jacobs. The specialist they called in to look at my father."

"I'm sorry, sir. There is no Dr. Jacobs on our roster."

"Are you sure?"

"Yes, I am. Are you all right?"

"I'm fine," I said, smiling.

"Thanks, Doc," I whispered.

Andrew Nichols
Grade 12
Highland View Academy
Hagerstown, Maryland

This story is a complex one. Telling a story primarily in flashbacks, as Andrew has done, is a difficult technique to manage. The movement in time is especially hard to handle here because a number of different times are involved. Beginning writers often take on tasks that are more complex than they are ready for simply because they don't yet know what is easy and what is hard!

Despite this, though, something happens here that

failed to happen in "Emergency!" or in Jenna's character sketch. We come to know who Jeff, the main character, is. In particular, we are given the history of Jeff's relationship with his father, which forms the core of the story's problem. And thus we understand his feelings and his motives as he faces his father's death.

Personal history is the most important single factor in bringing a character to life. When we understand the character's history with regard to the story problem, we understand his motives. We know *why* he feels as he does, acts as he does. Understanding, we usually share those feelings. At least we share them if the feelings are acted out, not just explained. And that is another reason we read stories, to be able to *feel* with the main character.

Go back through "Forgiveness" and note how much information Andrew has given us about Jeff's failed relationship with his father. Note, too, that he dramatizes the stronger moments, such as when Jeff and Sam are caught in the ambush. We live the events with Jeff. (The scene would be even stronger if the author hadn't told us what was going to happen with the somewhat clichéd reference to "the ultimate sacrifice" before he presented the scene.) He also plays out the conversation between Jeff and his father about Jeff's Distinguished Service Cross for valor, which is important to our understanding his feelings now. One piece of history supports and informs the other. Because we have lived through the battle scene with Jeff, we understand better his response to his father on the telephone. And, understanding, we care what happens to them both.

Characters—fully developed, believable, interesting

characters—form the heart of good fiction. Begin by knowing your characters' history as it affects the story problem. Learn to move inside a main character you know well, sharing his point of view—which is what we will be talking about in the next chapter—and your readers will be captured.

CHAPTER 6

Your Main Character's Point of View

The single most common reason stories fail is because the author hasn't moved deeply enough inside the main character. It is that perspective—looking out through your main character's eyes, hearing with his ears, thinking with his thoughts, feeling with his emotions—that brings a story to life.

Let's begin with the opening of a story that, although filled with action, never establishes the main character's point of view.

Baseball or Girls' Softball

Allison ran into the house and slammed the door shut. She threw her book bag across the floor and took off her coat and tossed it onto the couch. She raced up the stairs to her mother's, Laura's, room as if she were only an inch away from winning a marathon. She knocked on her mom's door so hard she was surprised that it didn't crack. The second her mom opened the door, she burst in and started rambling on about baseball sign-ups coming soon.

If she could type as fast as she talks, she would be an excellent secretary, her mom thought to herself.

Christen Dipetrillo
Grade 6
Montague Township Elementary School
Montague, New Jersey

I'll stop there. Look back at what has been presented. The author has given us a strong opening. Allison's excitement catches our attention. We know clearly that the story is going to be about Allison's wanting to sign up for baseball.

In the first paragraph, however, we never quite move inside Allison. We could be flies on the wall observing her excited entrance. The only moment when the author actually gets inside Allison's point of view is when she says, "She knocked on her mom's door so hard she was surprised that it didn't crack." Alison's surprise is internal. We move inside her to share it. But then in the next paragraph, we are in Allison's mother's point of view, sharing her thoughts about Allison's rush of excited talk.

Go back and reread those two paragraphs. What effect does observing Allison instead of being inside her have as the story begins? Do you feel connected with her yet, despite all her interesting excitement? And what happens to your interest in Allison when we step outside of her and look at her through her mother's eyes? Don't you find yourself feeling even more separated from her?

Some stories are written from an omniscient point of view. In these the writer stays in the background as an invisible narrator and tells us anything she wants us to

68

know about what is happening inside or outside each of the characters. But even in the hands of experienced writers, the reader is, inevitably, distanced from the main character by such a choice. And that distance will lose readers unless the writer knows exactly what she is doing.

Developing writers need to learn, first, to write from the point of view of a single character. Having learned that, there will be ample opportunity to experiment with more difficult choices.

Now let's consider another story, one in which the point of view remains clearly with the main character.

The Never-Ending Game

Hello. My name is Alex, and I'm going to tell you about a time when I got me and my friend into the biggest jam of all time. This happened about twenty— mmm, thirty years ago. I had just moved in so I didn't have any friends in Greenfield, Wisconsin. It was the summer of 1993, and it was about a week before school let out. It wasn't until later that I would make a friend and meet a girl who would change my life forever.

It started off like this. I was riding my bike around the complex I lived in when a kid with blond hair, black shorts, and a Shaq jersey on came walking toward me. I had no idea what he wanted, so I just thought I would play it cool. So I said, "What's up?"

He didn't answer. When he finally caught up to me he said, "Want to play baseball?"

I answered, "Sure, follow me."

We ran all the way to this little park. It really wasn't a park at all. In fact, we were still in the complex. It was more like a mini-field.

69

As I stepped onto the grass, I heard a voice call out. It said, "Hey, look at the little dweeb!"

I looked up. There were about six kids there.

"What did you say?" I asked.

A boy said, "I called you a dweeb, punk. What are you going to do about it?"

At this point I was really starting to get ticked off, so I started to walk toward him. "What did you say?" I decided to ask him once again.

"I called you a dweeb," he repeated again.

Without even thinking, I made a fist and put all my might into my punch. I took a swing—boom—and hit him square in the nose. The boy went down so fast that I didn't even know what I had done. I turned back and started to walk to my bike.

Suddenly all I heard was "Run!" coming from the kid in the Shaq jersey.

In a flash me and the kid in the Shaq jersey hopped on our bikes and were pedaling as fast as we could down the street. I had no idea where we were going, but I followed him anyway.

"What's your name?" I asked.

"Mike," he said. "What's yours?"

"Alex."

"Well, follow me, Alex," he called out to me. After a while we stopped right in front of somebody's front doorstep.

"Where are we, Mike?"

"Dina's house."

"Who's Dina?"

"Just somebody I used to know. Follow me. Be very quiet."

We tiptoed onto the front doorsteps of the house. I

didn't know what we were doing. But in an instant, he rang the doorbell.

"Run!" he shouted.

Once again without thinking I got on my bike and took off. This time he was following me. I could tell he didn't like it, because he kept pedaling harder and harder. But I didn't care. I just kept on pedaling.

After a while he yelled at me to stop. So we did.

"Who's Dina? And why did you do that?" I asked.

"Okay, look, Alex. Me and Dina used to be friends. Then she started to get really mean and mad all the time, so we started drifting apart. After that we became enemies." Mike looked around. "Ah, you know what? Dina has a bee gun. All cool. Want it?"

"What do you mean, want it?"

"Alex, wake up. I mean to go into her garage and take it."

I didn't want to look stupid by saying no, so I said, "Sure."

"Then follow me," he said.

So we started pedaling again toward Dina's house. We stopped right in front of Dina's garage. It was open, and I could see the gun lying there on a chair that was in the middle of the garage. Mike said, "Okay. Go get it, Alex."

"I'm not getting it. You go get it."

"Fine. I'll go get it." He stepped onto the cement of the garage and walked over to where the gun was sitting. He picked it up, then dropped it on the ground and ran out of the garage. He looked at me and said, "I can't do it, Alex. Let's go."

He must have decided to try again, because he stepped back into the garage and walked toward the gun. He began to pick it up, but once again he dropped it and began to run out of the garage.

He looked at me again and said, "Okay. This time I'm going to do it."

He stepped into the garage and walked toward the gun. He picked it up and started running. Both of us ran to our bikes as fast as we could. Then we were off speeding away on our bikes. I followed him into some kind of forest.

We stopped in what looked like some sort of a ditch, and I told him, "We shouldn't have done it, Mike."

"I asked you," he answered, "and you said sure. Remember?"

"Well, now I want out," I said.

He stared at me and calmly said, "Sorry, but you can't get out. You try it and see what happens to you."

"Oh, all right," I mumbled. "Just don't tell anybody. I have to go. See you."

After that day I knew this wasn't a game anymore. We were thieves, and if we were caught we could get into serious trouble. From that day on my heart never stopped pounding with fear.

"I have to tell Dad," I kept thinking. I rode my bike home. When I got there my dad's car was parked in the driveway, so I went up to talk to him. "Ah, son. Ready for lunch?" he asked.

"Dad, I thought you were at work" was all I could say.

"I came home on my lunch break. Oh yeah, son, do you know somebody named Dina?"

I felt like I was going to have a heart attack.

I spoke as calmly as possible. "I've heard of her."

"Well, somebody stole her bee gun."

"Really?"

"Yes. The manager told me all about it when I went to pay the rent. Oh yeah, he also wanted me to ask you if you saw anybody suspicious hanging around here lately."

"No, not really."

"All right. Well, lunch will be ready in a little bit."

"Ah, Dad? What if somebody stole that gun but really didn't mean any harm and was going to return it?"

"Do you know something, son?"

"No, I was just wondering."

"They would probably go to court if the mother or father wanted to press charges."

"Then what would happen to the person who stole it?"

"They would have to pay whatever Dina's parents sued them for, son. Is there something wrong?" he asked me again.

"No. I'm just curious."

"You know you can tell me anything, don't you, son?"

"Yeah, Dad, but nothing is wrong. Dad, I'm going outside for a while. Okay?"

"Hurry up. Lunch is going to be done in a little bit."

So I went outside and got on my bike. I rode it to where Dina's house was. I had decided to tell Dina's parents the truth. When I rang the doorbell, I could tell they were expecting somebody because they answered the door in an instant.

"Hello, my name is Alex. I heard you had your gun stolen."

"Yeah, it was my gun."

"Dina, I thought you were watching TV," her mother said with surprise.

"Sorry, Mom. I couldn't stop thinking about my bee gun."

"Why is it so important to you?" came bursting out of my mouth.

"My grandfather gave it to me. It's been in the family for years. It's an antique. It's really the only thing I have to remember him by."

"Oh, I've got to go. My dad's waiting for me."

"All right. Bye."

When I was riding my bike home I had an idea. I would get the gun and leave it on her doorstep. Then I wouldn't get into trouble and nobody would have to know. So I went to the forest where we hid it. When I got up to it there was a log on top of it. A tree must have fallen down on it.

I hoped it would be all right. So I dug up the earth under it so I could get it free. I felt a part of the gun so I pulled it out. When I saw it, my heart skipped about one hundred beats. Half of the gun was torn off. The tree must have broken it when it fell. Now, I knew I had to tell my dad. So I grabbed the gun and started heading home.

I opened the door to my house.

"You're back," came my father's voice from somewhere inside.

"Yeah, Dad. Oh, Dad? I have to tell you something."

"What is it, son?"

"You know Dina's gun. I'm the one who stole it. I'm sorry, Dad. This kid really hated her, so he thought we should steal her gun."

"You're in big trouble."

"What's going to happen to me, Dad?"

"You're going to give the gun back."

"But it's broken, Dad, see?"

74

"Then we're going to get it fixed, and you're going to pay for it out of your own allowance. You're also grounded for a month."

After that day, Mike never talked to me again, because my dad called his parents and told them all about it, too. But I didn't care, because I was happy it was all over. Besides, I could make other friends who wouldn't get me into trouble this time.

Mark A. Lopez
Grade 5
Glenwood Elementary School
Greenfield, Wisconsin

There is much that this story does well. The author lays out the background as to why Alex would go along with the idea of stealing the gun: he is new in town and without friends, and Mike has helped him out of a scrape. The tension rises as the situation keeps getting worse. Alex's father knows about the theft and mentions it. In fact, he talks about how serious the consequences will be. The gun turns out to be irreplaceable, because it was a gift from Dina's grandfather and the only thing she has left from him. It is found broken when Alex tries to go back to retrieve it.

One suggestion I would make to Mark would be that he start right into the present action of the story instead of beginning with Alex's talking from thirty years into the future. This would give the story a more immediate impact.

A more important issue remains, however. We are consistently in Alex's point of view because this is a first-person narrative. But even though we remain solidly in Alex's perspective, he reveals nothing of his own thoughts and feelings, except for the times when he mentions his heart "pounding with fear" or "skipp[ing] about one hundred beats."

The action—and the basis for it—is so clear that it is easy to guess what Alex is thinking and feeling at each moment. What, for instance, does he think about Mike when Mike comes to his rescue the way he does? What is he feeling when Mike wants him to go into the garage to steal the gun? When Mike himself does it? When Alex's dad tells him what the consequences will be?

This is a good story to use for discovering ways to reveal the main character's thoughts, feelings, and sensory impressions. Rewrite the fight scene, for instance. Explore Alex's thoughts when he is called a "dweeb." What does his fist feel like when it makes contact with the other boy's nose? How does his body react as he pedals away?

Look for other scenes to rewrite. This story has many strong moments in which Alex's inner world could be explored. How does Alex feel when Mike steals the gun? When his father talks about the consequences that lie in wait for whoever stole it? When he discovers how important the gun is to Dina?

Alex would experience the world through his senses, too. What does the forest look like, sound like, smell like when Alex reaches it? Does it feel quiet and safe? Does a squirrel chatter from a tree, and does the squirrel seem to be accusing him of the theft? Use your imagination. Climb inside Alex. Bring him to life. Make a good story stronger.

Here is another story, this one in the third person, in which the author succeeds in revealing the main character's point of view. As you read it, take note of the character's feelings and the way we experience the world through her senses.

Lean on Me

"Turn down that music, Steve!" said Carrie from the back seat of his blue Pinto.

Alyssa poked her head around the passenger seat she was occupying to look at Carrie. "Just chill, okay?" Alyssa coaxed. The three acquaintances were tense as they drove home for Christmas break from college over slippery roads and through near-blizzard conditions.

Carrie just gave her an annoyed look and moved closer to the window. She leaned her head against the seat and closed her eyes. *Why can't anyone be nice to me anymore?* she thought. *Nobody cares about me now that my parents are gone.*

Surrounded by darkness, except for the gentle light of the dashboard and headlights, she cried, remembering the night she received the news of her parents' deaths six months ago. As she gazed out the window, she tried to ignore the empty feeling of anguish in the pit of her stomach. She was jolted back to reality when the car began to swerve on the slippery county road.

"Slow down!" Carrie shouted.

"Whoa!" giggled Alyssa.

"We're fine," Steve said assuredly. "You want to be dropped off at your aunt and uncle's place on time for Christmas, don't you, Carrie?"

"Not especially," Carrie murmured under her breath.

The memories of past Christmases with her parents

drifted into her thoughts. Life had been so wonderful before her parents died, but now she was filled with apprehension about how it would be with her aunt and uncle. Was she merely a responsibility, or did her rich relatives really want her with them?

Suddenly their speeding car swerved to the right and continued skidding as Steve fought in vain for control of the car. Before any of them knew what was happening, the car began rolling into the ditch and came to an abrupt halt . . . upside-down!

There was dead silence; exactly what Carrie was afraid of. They might be dead.

"Are you two okay?" Carrie uttered anxiously.

There was a long pause before Steve replied. "Yep. I think we'll stop here!"

A surge of relief swept through her, even though they weren't particularly close friends.

"Alyssa, are you okay?" she asked apprehensively.

After a moment's pause, Alyssa responded, "I think so."

A small sigh escaped Carrie's lips. She slowly and painfully unbuckled her seat belt and fell awkwardly onto the roof of the car.

Her hand fumbled in the darkness to find the handle that would release the door. She slowly stood up, caught her balance in the upside-down car, and crawled out.

"Well, are you two going to just sit there, or are you going to get out?" Carrie questioned impatiently. The wind lashed at her face as she waited for their response. "I don't know about you, but I'm moving on, even if it's the last thing I do!" . . .

[The three argue about what they should do until Steve finally takes over.]

"Come on. Let's go, ladies. Follow me!" commanded Steve as he turned to lead them in the direction he obviously thought they should go.

"That's the wrong way, Steve," Carrie countered. "We have to follow the road. It's really starting to snow hard now. We don't want to get lost."

Carrie was sure that the road would lead them to safety, but since she was new to the area, she reluctantly agreed to follow Steve's shortcut. "Fine," yelled Carrie.

Carrie's thoughts turned on herself. *Oh, why are we fighting again?* she thought. *I'm always fighting with everyone lately. No, they started it. See if I ever ride with them again!*

As they trudged on through the knee-deep snow and harsh winds, they grew tired, and the arguing only intensified.

"We can't keep going," complained Alyssa breathlessly. "I need to rest!"

"All right, we'll stop for a moment," Steve offered. "Do you feel better when we stop?" Steve asked tenderly.

"Yeah. I'll be fine. Thanks," replied Alyssa.

Carrie turned away from the two as a pang of jealousy gripped her. *Why doesn't anyone ever talk to me that way?* Carrie wondered. *Why do I seem to push people away these days? The last six months have been so hard. I wish I had someone to comfort me!*

Carrie swallowed hard and suggested that they get started making a shelter for the night.

"We need to make a fire, too," Alyssa announced as though she had surprised herself with the sensible idea.

"I'll go find some wood," said Steve. "I think I saw a

patch of trees back along the road somewhere."

"No, I need you here to help me dig the shelter," Carrie said, hoping that maybe Steve would consider staying with her.

"*Dig* the shelter?" Steve questioned in disbelief. "You mean you want to actually dig a hole in the snow?"

"Yeah, what would you suggest?" Carrie barked, suddenly feeling angry and hurt by Steve's lack of compassion toward her. "Do you think we should build it out of wood and make a few hundred trips back to the woods you supposedly saw? We don't even know if there are any trees around here. We can't trust you anymore. You're the one who got us into this mess in the first place!" Carrie said as she fought back tears.

"Stop it, you two!" Alyssa reprimanded.

Ashamed, Carrie muttered to Steve, "Sorry."

"Me, too," Steve mumbled.

[Steve does go off to look for wood, and Carrie and Alyssa proceed to dig a shelter in the snow. During the process they come to be friends. After some time passes, however, they grow concerned because Steve hasn't returned.]

Soon, Carrie's anxiety got the best of her. She asked Alyssa to give her a boost and went out to search for Steve. Carrie shielded her eyes and looked around at the endless mounds of snow. After several chilling minutes, Carrie heard footsteps behind her. Overjoyed, she yelped and turned to greet Steve. When she pivoted, though, she saw nothing.

An eerie feeling shot through her body. She turned sharply to find four pairs of amber eyes peering back at her. Carrie screamed as the wolves became suddenly more visible from over one of the hills of snow. They

80

started moving closer to her. The wolves seemed to be more curious than hungry. She ran full speed toward their shelter, trying not to make the location of their shelter too obvious. Carrie leaped into the shelter, and together she and Alyssa huddled in the corner. They barely dared breathe. The girls watched as the wolves poked their heads into the hole to investigate. Then, as suddenly as they had come, they disappeared.

Carrie remained frozen, huddled next to Alyssa for a long time before she felt brave enough to move. Eventually, she relaxed and caught her breath.

[Steve returns. The three light a fire and spend the night in their snow shelter, growing closer in understanding as they face each challenge.]

"We just might make it, after all," Alyssa said rather flatly, and her blue eyes showed a glimmer of hope. Carrie reached out to squeeze her friend's hand.

"Of course we will," Carried reassured her. "We're in this together, and if I have any say in it, we're going to be safe at home in no time!"

Carrie looked up to find Steve looking curiously and admiringly at her. She looked down at her hands, folded in her lap, and wondered herself what had caused her change in attitude. As she watched their shadows dance on the walls from the cozy fire, she felt courage, hope and happiness for the first time since her parents had died. Determination had replaced her former feelings of confusion, bitterness, and exaggerated independence. Her visions of forbidding, treacherous snow now seemed like an invitation to adventure....

Steve awakened them the next morning by dropping small snowballs on their faces. Alyssa and Carrie screamed and threw snow back at Steve. The morning sunlight lit up the sparkling white shelter. The calm, bright, blue sky withheld the many mysteries of the new day.

"I want my bacon and eggs!" Steve whined jokingly.

"I'm thirsty," Alyssa added.

Carrie responded, "Our food's almost gone, and we can't eat snow." Then suddenly she blurted, "That's it!"

"What's it?" Alyssa demanded anxiously.

Carrie answered, "We can melt the snow in our pop cans over the fire!"

"Smart thinking, Carrie!" Steve cheered.

When they had all but exhausted their food supply and drunk their water, they packed up and said "good-bye" to their shelter. They headed off in the warm sunlight toward the road. A long period of time passed before the three voiced their fears. Had they come this far in the wrong direction?

Alyssa sat down heavily on the ground and cried, "How could this have happened? Nothing looks familiar!"

"It was dark out when we traveled last night," Carrie said. "Maybe we're not lost. I'm sure we came from this way."

"You know, I think she's right," Steve replied.

Carrie continued hopefully, "I think we should just walk along this strip here for a while. Maybe we're just a little off."

They pressed on with only a few rests here and there. Suddenly Alyssa stopped abruptly.

"Listen," she panted.

Faint voices could be heard nearby. Steve's, Carrie's, and Alyssa's cries rang clearly through the crisp winter air.

"We did it, you two," Carrie explained. "They

found our car! We were right! We did it together!"

They used what little energy they had left to run toward the voices. There were police, Carrie's aunt and uncle, Alyssa's mom, and Steve's dad, all talking nervously. Carrie ran up to her aunt and uncle to embrace them.

Carrie turned around to smile at her friends who had helped her through this nightmare. Yet now, as she looked back at the dazzling snow, Caribbean sea-blue sky, and fluffy clouds, she could think only of the fond memories and an overall experience that had truly changed her life.

She no longer lived in the past, but instead, she had learned to look forward to the happy times ahead of her.

Marisa Martinson
Grade 7
Osseo Junior High School
Osseo, Minnesota

What a fine job Marisa has done of letting us share her main character's thoughts, of experiencing the world through her senses! At almost every moment we know what Carrie is thinking and feeling. She reacts to everything that is going on, not just to the accident and to the cold world the three find themselves in, but to her own past and to Steve and Alyssa, too. When Carrie goes out to look for Steve, we experience the "endless mounds of snow" and the "four pairs of amber eyes peering back at her." And because we have been inside Carrie throughout, we accept and share the change of heart she has at the end. We, too, look forward to the happy times ahead, because we have been part of her change.

Some aspects of "Lean on Me" could use work. A few times Marisa moves out of Carrie's point of view and tells us what everyone is thinking and feeling. The last sentence of the second paragraph of the story is a case in point. Each time that happens, readers are pushed back, losing contact with Carrie, if only momentarily.

Beyond that minor point, though, is a larger one. Beginning writers often tend to reach for the most dramatic, even melodramatic, material. In this story the idea of Carrie's having been recently orphaned smacks of melodrama. There is no rule that says you can't use such a plot idea, but emotionally traumatic material such as this is extremely difficult to handle well.

The story might also be more interesting if Carrie's alienation could have a more subtle cause. What if she is on scholarship and the other two come from families with money, so she doesn't feel as if she is really part of them? What if she has recently broken up with her longtime boyfriend and thinks that nothing which remains has any value? What if . . . but you come up with other alternatives.

Whether Carrie's issues are large or small, however, the key is to climb inside her and explore them . . . exactly as Marisa has done here.

Look with your main character's eyes. Hear with her ears. Think with her thoughts. Feel with her feelings.

Your story will come to life!

Or at least it will if this character is involved in an interesting struggle. And struggle is what we will discuss next.

CHAPTER 7

Struggle, the Secret of Story

We all know what a story is. At least we can all identify a story when we see one. Creating a story ourselves can be another matter entirely. Many of the manuscripts I see from young writers are lively, well written, and deeply felt, but they are not stories.

A while back I received the following letter from a young writer:

Dear Marion,

Hi! I'm a kid writer. I'm eleven years old and I have strawberry-blond hair and too many freckles. Writing stories is one of my gifts. I guess that's why I was so interested in your book, *What's Your Story?* But I wanted to show you just how much the book helped me improve my writing skills.

The first story enclosed is called "Stanley Swimmer." I wrote it about a year ago for a school project. You can plainly see there is no descriptive language or anything that would be interesting. It's really pretty boring and there's nothing to learn from it.

The next story, "A Visit with My Attic Friends" was written recently *after* I read your writing book. I feel inspired when I read it over again and I feel so good because I actually wrote a story that I enjoy reading myself.

I've started a writers' group for kids. We just got together for the first time yesterday. It went over good. Everybody there liked to write and some volunteered to read parts of their stories. I read "A Visit with My Attic Friends" to them and the compliments poured in. It made me feel like I'd really accomplished something.

Thanks for all the help your book gave me. I know it'll change my writing life in a big good way. Just wanted to share that with you!

Sincerely with good writings,
Suzanne Van Rijn
Kid Writer

Suzanne asked me not to print the first story she sent, "Stanley Swimmer," but she gave me permission to use "A Visit with My Attic Friends." Here it is.

A Visit with My Attic Friends

It was true, I had too many dolls. I looked at them standing motionless on the wooden shelves of the attic. One was lifting a pink cup to her mouth, another was rocking a cradle. But they all were still, as if they had suddenly frozen in the middle of their activities. But among them, I loved only one. Her name was Mary.

I had seen her first, sitting in a store window with all the other Christmas decor. She had been dressed in a real red velvet dress! A green bow was tied around her waist and one like it was tied in her dark molasses hair.

"Daddy?" I had asked, stopping to eye the china doll.

But I needn't say more. Daddy picked me up in his strong arms and said, "Well, after all, it's almost Christmas!" his warm blue eyes gleaming.

When December 25th came it was a chilly morning and outside snow had collected on the window panes. My sister was up first and like a lady put on her robe and slippers. But me? I ran down barefoot without a care in the world!

There was Mary sitting under the bright tree. I didn't even notice Ben's bright new train or Cara's beautiful purple tea set. All I wanted was Mary!

"Every night from now on you'll get to sleep in Cara's and my room," I had said, feeling how cold her body was. "I'll even make a little bed for you on the vanity."

But now Mary stood on the shelf with the other dolls. I felt maybe I'd neglected her. I reached for her delicate china body, but then stopped. Mary had been one of my child things. We had been best of friends and favorite tea-party companions, but it was all my imagination that she had feelings and wasn't just another doll.

I turned the lamp off and left them in the peaceful silhouette light just as the first flake of snow fell onto the attic window. Curled up in Daddy's big old chair, I fell asleep, watching the flakes wisp through the chilly wind. I never noticed Mary watching me from the corner of the room.

Suzanne Van Rijn
Grade 5
Lincoln School
Corona del Mar, California

The most important response to this story is Suzanne's own—that she can go back to it and read it with enjoyment. And the reasons the story works for her are many.

The descriptive language is good. Can't you see the doll, Mary? Perhaps even more important, the narrator's emotional connection with the doll comes through strongly. The narrator's feelings toward her father come through clearly, too, without her ever talking about them. Whether she is being lifted in Daddy's strong arms or curling up in his big old chair, we feel how important her father is to her. And the connection with her father is part of her connection with the doll as well.

The final sentence, a contradiction of all the narrator's mature acceptance of the doll as just another "child thing," sends an intriguing chill down the spine. "I never noticed Mary watching me from the corner of the room."

All of this is a fine setup for a story. I wouldn't be surprised if Suzanne finds the story hidden in this description one day. But at this point, it is not yet a story.

What would it take to turn Suzanne's appealing personal memoir into a story? Struggle. The main character would need to struggle either to get the doll or, perhaps more likely given the theme of the memoir, to put the doll behind her. What if a girl has outgrown a doll who refuses to be outgrown? How might the doll pursue her? What might the girl do to get free? Or might she struggle to get free, only to decide in the end that this connection with her child self isn't so bad, after all?

Think about the groundwork Suzanne has laid. Does any part of this memoir suggest an actual story to you, one in which the main character struggles to achieve some goal?

Here is another authentic experience from a young writer, this one played out more fully than "A Visit with My Attic Friends." As you read, ask yourself, is "Friends Forever" a fully developed story?

Friends Forever

The end of the year Carnival was going to be in one hour, and I couldn't wait. I tried to sit still, but there was *no way* that was going to be possible. I kept jumping up and down, up and down, thinking of stuff to do.

Finally, I called Sandie. She lives across the street, and she's my best friend. She was probably acting like I was. I was right.

"Hi, it's me," I said after she said hello.

"Alicia, hi. Are you as jumpy as I am? I jumped when the phone rang!" Sandie said with a giggle.

"Yes, I am. I feel like a frog!" I replied, and we both started laughing.

"Hey, Sandie," I said, "come over. Then we can jump around together."

"Good idea," she answered. "Bye!" And she hung up.

In a couple of minutes, she was on the doorstep. The air was muggy and hot, and it felt a little too warm.

"Come in," I told Sandie. "There's an air conditioner inside." And I pulled her inside.

We were wearing almost identical outfits. We like dressing alike. Most people don't like doing that, but we think it's cool.

"Come on," Sandie suggested. "We'll be early, but I can't wait any longer, can you?"

"No, I think I'll explode with excitement. Let's go!"
I called. We thumped down the stairs.

We walked a little way until we could see Long
Beach Junior High, our school. We normally walk to
school because we live so close. At last I couldn't walk
any longer.

"Last one to the school is a ROTTEN EGG!" I
yelled, and we took off. We were running so fast I felt
the breeze gently sting my face. My ponytail was bop-
ping up and down. I was getting out of breath. We were
getting very close. We were neck and neck. And . . .
"You're a rotten egg!" we both called in unison. We
laughed. We'd tied!

We walked inside the school. It was barely cooler
than outside. All that body heat! We strolled around
into and out of rooms that looked interesting. But one
in particular sparked my attention. It had beads dan-
gling down the door. The sign said "Fortune Telling"
and had a picture of a crystal ball on it.

"I think I'll go in here," I said. "Want to come?"

"No, thanks. I'll wait," Sandie replied.

"Okey-dokey," I said.

I walked in cautiously. The room was dim, and a
short line waited impatiently to see "Ms. Guinivere,
The Great Gypsy" in a smaller room.

When it was my turn, I walked in slowly and looked
around. There was Lady Guinivere. She had a white
turban on her head and a jingly beaded shawl covering
a skin-tight white dress. She had dark rouge blush and
darker eye make-up. She was made up great.

"Sit down," she said with a Transylvanian accent.

I sat down.

"Your name?" Guinivere asked.

"Alicia Pierce," I replied in a whisper. I was dumbfounded. I hoped she didn't expect me to talk much. I was afraid that I wouldn't be able to. I was lucky.

"Well, I'm Lady Guinivere, Alicia," she said, rolling her "r." "Now, don't be afraid. I don't bite." And she stared into her crystal ball.

"I'm getting it, getting it," she called quietly, making me edge forward. "Someone close, verrry close to you is moving farrr, farrr away. Somewhere you've nev-err been before. I'm losing it . . . it's gone. I must rrrest," she said with her hand over her head.

Then, another gypsy wearing all black escorted me out, and I got a jawbreaker. It was very weird.

"How did it go?" asked Sandie.

"Weird," I replied, and I told her what Lady Guinivere had said. "Strange, isn't it?" I said, popping the jawbreaker into my mouth.

"Yeah," said Sandie uncomfortably.

I wondered what was wrong. Oh well.

We wandered around, and I won some soda pop. Sandie's purse was full of candy. She wasn't the same all night. When the principal came on the P.A. system wishing us a happy summer and everyone cheered, she barely clapped her hands.

We walked home in silence.

"See you tomorrow," I told Sandie. We planned to go to the beach and get some ice cream afterwards.

"Yeah, bye," she replied and ran up her front stoop.

What was with her, anyway? I went home and slept, tossing and turning.

When I woke up, I remembered the beach and just couldn't get cheered. The way Sandie acted kept popping into my head. Something bad was going to happen that day. I just didn't know what.

I grabbed some granola bars and made some sandwiches. I wrote a note and stuck it to the fridge and left.

I was just about to ring the bell when Sandie came out. Grabbing her bag she said, "Come on, let's hit the beach!"

"All right," I told her. "Let's go!"

We walked in silence part of the way until I couldn't stand it any longer.

"Sandie, what was wrong with you last night?"

"I was . . . uh . . . tired," she stuttered.

Finally, we got to the beach. We stripped down and spread out our towels. We waded in the waves. Soon we were splashing each other and laughing. We were racing each other, and Sandie swam way faster than I did. We ate and listened to music. We had a lot of fun. We didn't want to leave when the lifeguards left.

We gathered our stuff and headed to the ice-cream shop. Sandie ordered a milk shake, and I ordered a two-scoop cone of chocolate ice cream.

"Um . . . I need to . . . um . . . tell you something," said Sandie.

"Yeah?" I said, taking a bite of my ice cream.

"I'm moving . . . to Massachusetts," said Sandie. "I'm leaving in three days. I just couldn't tell you. I'm sorry."

She looked close to tears. I nearly choked.

"What?" I whispered. "My fortune was right!" I exclaimed, flabbergasted. "In three days?" I repeated.

She nodded. We finished our ice cream in silence. We walked home rarely saying anything. I felt like someone just knocked the wind out of me. My best friend was moving to MASSACHUSETTS!

I went home and went to my room. I put on some

dry clothes and brushed my hair. When dinnertime came, I told everyone.

"Guess what?" I asked.

"What? What?" answered Thomas.

"The Youngs are moving to Massachusetts," I answered glumly.

"Where's Mathatoothets?" asked Thomas.

"Oh, down the road about four thousand miles," joked Joanne.

Then she came back to reality. "Jessica," whispered Joanne. Jessica is Sandie's sister.

"Ross," whispered Thomas. Ross is Thomas's friend and Sandie's brother.

"Sandie," my parents whispered.

I nodded. Everyone likes Sandie's family, but I am the only one who is BEST FRIENDS.

We ate the rest of the meal quietly.

Moving day came, and I didn't want to get up, but I did. I got dressed and ran down the stairs.

Everyone was waiting. "Let's get it over with," I told everyone. We went over to their house.

"Come into my room," Sandie said. I followed her down the hall. No family pictures hung on the walls. Sandie's room was bare. The movers were ready to load everything up, and they did it too fast. Everyone said goodbye.

"I guess this is it," I said.

"I guess," said Sandie.

"Goodbye," I replied.

"Bye," called Sandie.

"Friends forever?" I asked.

"Friends forever!" Sandie replied tearfully.

We didn't have to remind each other to call and

write, because I knew we would. When they drove away, I started crying, and I ran back to the house. I sat on my bed for hours, clutching my pillow. I don't remember my family coming home, but I knew that they did.

Mom came up to my room and held me. We didn't say anything. We just sat. I'll miss Sandie a lot. She is a great friend.

Kasi DeLaPorte
Grade 4
Wayside Elementary School
Bartlesville, Oklahoma

Again, this story is written with clear, strong feelings, feelings readers can share. It is also played out in good detail. (The details are, in fact, so thoroughly played out that I eliminated some of them, especially about the girls' clothing, to keep the story moving.) But we share the significant moments, such as when Alicia is warned that someone important is going to move and, again, when she finds out that the person is Sandie. We don't have to be told that Sandie is special to Alicia, either. Seeing the two girls together is enough to tell us that. However, in spite of the clear and significant problem presented here, we still have a situation, not a story.

What would be needed to make "Friends Forever" a story? Again . . . struggle. The main character, Alicia, needs to struggle to do something about her problem, the discovery that her best friend, Sandie, is moving.

Now, realistically, there isn't a lot a girl can do about her friend's parents' decision to move to another state. But she could still try to make a difference. Maybe she and Sandie together might come up with a plan

94

designed to change Sandie's parents' minds. Or they might attempt to prevent Sandie's father or mother from being accepted in the new job that is causing them to move. Or Alicia might get angry at Sandie for not fighting the move, deciding Sandie doesn't really care about the friendship. In the end, probably none of these struggles would change the situation. It is Alicia, herself, who would have to change. But if she has struggled, we would then be prepared for her change of heart.

"Friends Forever" is a good length for a short story as it stands. Would Kasi need to develop her story into a novel in order to include a struggle? No. If she set up the problem (Sandie's impending move) at the beginning instead of using most of the story to lead into it, she would have ample space for Alicia to react.

While the opening, with all of the girls' excitement over the Carnival, is appealing, the Carnival isn't the point. The fortune Alicia hears is the point. So perhaps the story could begin as the girls walk to the Carnival, filled with excitement and camaraderie, revealing what good friends they are. Then the scene could turn immediately to the fortune-teller.

Instead of having Sandie act uncomfortable but say nothing when the fortune is revealed, Alicia's fortune could lead much more directly to the truth. We wouldn't need the whole beach scene just to lead up to Sandie's revelation. Then Alicia would be ready to launch into her struggle . . . whatever it is. And Alicia's struggle would be the core of the story.

You might want to try to rewrite "Friends Forever." Compress the early information and get right into Alicia's attempt to do something about the problem.

Real life is filled with situations about which we can

do nothing, exactly like the one Kasi has presented here. If a real-life situation is to become a story, however, the main character must take charge of the outcome. She may succeed in changing the situation, or she may succeed only in changing herself. But it is her struggle that will pull the reader in.

Here is a full-fledged story, one in which the main character does struggle and resolve her own problem.

The Proving Project

"Elyse never got in trouble. Why do you?"

"Elyse never got D's. Why can't you be more like Elyse?"

I don't know why my parents are so surprised on report-card day. By now you'd think they would be used to my failing grades. I've only been getting them for the past three years.

I picked up my bookbag and headed to Carly Haven's house. Carly has been my best friend practically forever. We had gotten a big Social Studies assignment, and I was going to work on it at Carly's house. Mrs. Haven is an artist, and she has a ton of supplies.

Usually, I don't get too involved in schoolwork, but this one wasn't just for the grade. I was finally going to prove that I was not Elyse Bennett.

"Yo, Josey!" Roy called out. He lives a few houses away from Carly. He and a bunch of boys from my class were sitting on Roy's front steps.

"What?" I asked, jogging up his lawn.

"Want to play football with us?" Roy asked.

"Nah. I've got to start my family tree," I answered.

"Josey, are you feeling okay?" he asked skeptically.

"Yeah," I replied.

"But you always play with us," Randy joined in. "You said yourself you'd rather hang out with us than do school stuff."

"I know. But this is different." I gave a quick wave and dashed off.

At dinner that night I tried not to act unusual. When my mother asked how school was, I gave the usual remark. "It stunk." I patiently listened to Elyse brag about how well she was doing in her senior year and how she was positive she would graduate at the top of her class.

"Mrs. Haven called before. She said something about a family-tree project. How's it coming?" my mom asked.

"It's not coming. I'm not going to do it," I replied.

"Why am I not surprised?" my father mumbled to himself.

"That's your choice," my mom said. "If only you were—"

"More like Elyse." I finished her sentence. "May I be excused?" I asked.

The next afternoon, I went over to Carly's house to work on my project. When she answered the door, I could tell something was up. When she told me that her little sister, Hannah, had spilled apple juice all over my project, I could have killed her.

"What?" I hissed, not wanting to believe what she had just said.

"It was an accident. Hannah just wandered down-stairs."

I didn't want to lose my best friend, so I just said, "Fine. Take a deep breath, count to three, and walk away." I turned around and started to walk home.

"Weird," Carly muttered. She shook her head and closed the door.

I walked home, depressed. It was just my luck. I finally get involved in a school project and it gets ruined. My last chance to do this stupid project was to stay after school every day and work on it in the after-school program.

The next afternoon, I worked by myself, plotting out, sketching, drawing, erasing, and starting over. By the end of the afternoon, I had put on the finishing touches and was ready to hand in my masterpiece the next day.

I ran home as fast as I could. I burst into the house. It was a good thing my mom was home from work today, because I don't think I would have lasted much longer.

"How was school?" my mom asked.

"See for yourself," I said proudly, thrusting the poster board at her.

"Josey, I'm so proud of you!" my mom shrieked. "Why did you say you weren't going to do it?"

"So you'd be surprised. Do you think I did better than Elyse did when she was my age?" The last question had slipped.

"Oh. So that's what it is. You did this so that you could prove that you and Elyse are equal," she said, sounding disappointed.

"Technically, yes," I admitted.

"Josey, we know you're not Elyse. I promise to try to stop comparing you two all the time. But—"

"There's always a catch," I cut in.

"Just listen, please," my mom continued. "Only if you promise to try a little harder."

"I promise. I'll try to try," I said.

Maybe things were finally going to change around here.

Jessica Hermo
Grade 6
Montague Elementary School
Montague, New Jersey

In "The Proving Project" the main character stays in charge of the action. She struggles all the way through. And she is the one who brings the situation to a resolution. Josey's struggle takes a traditional story shape: attempt, failure, attempt, near failure, success.

Jessica does a fine job of revealing Josey's character through the dialogue, the conversations both with her parents and with the boys. When her father mumbles, "Why am I not surprised?" we get an instant summation of a great many family battles as well as a clear indication of her parents' attitude toward her. When Randy says, "You said yourself you'd rather hang out with us than do school stuff," we can guess a great deal about Josey.

Further aspects of the story could use work. The resolution may, finally, be too easy. Why, after all, has Josey chosen this moment and this project to compete with her sister's sterling record? Also, Josey's reason for deciding to do the family tree project is unclear. She says, "I was finally going to prove that I was not Elyse Bennett," but can Josey prove she is not her sister by excelling in the same way her sister does? Probably she does the project to prove that she is just as good as her perfect older sister.

Still, the author has a story here. She has a character who struggles and who achieves what she sets out to get

. . . a change in her parents' attitude toward her.

In real life we are not always in charge of the outcome of our own stories. Often we don't even try to be. And that is another important reason that people read fiction in the first place, to see the main character take charge and do something about her problem. When we become part of that character's struggle, we, ourselves, feel empowered.

Beginning writers often create main characters who sit around thinking deep and mournful thoughts about their problems. These writers are on exactly the right track to start off with a *problem*. What they forget, however, is that it isn't the character's *problem* that makes a story. It is her *struggle* to find a solution for the problem.

Your main character must attempt to do something about the problem she faces. She may do the wrong things. All of her action may come to nothing except a new acceptance, an inner change. But she must remain in charge. She must act and react to the story problem from beginning to end.

Action alone, however, won't make a story. Beneath the action there must be a person, a person who feels.

In the next chapter we will examine feelings—your characters' feelings and your readers' also.

CHAPTER 8

Making Your Readers Feel

W hy do human beings love stories? On paper, in films, told around campfires? I have already proposed several answers to that question.

Every single person sometimes feels isolated, alone. Discovering ourselves in a character, we break through that isolation.

Another reason we read stories is that we all have had the experience of facing a problem we didn't believe we could change. When a story's main character struggles and makes a difference, we, too, feel empowered.

Most important of all, however, we seek out stories, even scary stories or sad stories or fantasies we know couldn't actually happen, because we like to feel. We especially enjoy experiencing strong feelings when we can do so without risking our own limbs and psyches. And stories give us a chance to feel in perfect safety.

Your most crucial task when you set out to write a story is to make your readers feel. But how do you do that?

You start off with a story problem that is important. Important to one person: your main character. The best stories are rarely about big issues, nations at war, the destruction of rain forests, plagues. The best stories almost always explore smaller, more personal problems. If your main character cares passionately about getting on the swim team, your readers will care about her getting on the swim team, too. At least your readers will care if you give them a chance to understand and share your main character's feelings.

Here is a story where the protagonist is confronted by a problem that could hardly be more important to him. His life, after all, is on the line. Do you care about his problem, too, as you read? Do you feel it with him?

Frank and the Grizzly

It was five o'clock in the morning. The air smelled clean and fresh. Everything was silent except the sound of crunching snow under the snowshoes of Frank Gifferd and the sound of his Alaskan malamute, Bo, panting behind.

It was pitch black. Frank flipped on the flashlight that he held in his hand. He quickly shone the flashlight about ten yards in front of him. The sight was gruesome. There was blood splattered all around the trap and large footprints leading away with splotches of blood alongside of them. There was still a leg of the lynx that had been caught in the trap just an hour before.

"Drats!" Frank yelled. "That grizzly got my lynx again."

He stood still, listening, but everything was silent. Then all of a sudden, "CRACK!" A loud sound echoed through the woodland. Bo began to bark as Frank unholstered the .41 magnum Black-hawk from his hip.

"Something's running at us," Frank said to nobody but his dog Bo.

Frank quickly cocked the .41 magnum that he held in his hand and pointed the pistol into the air and slowly squeezed the trigger. The loud bang echoed through the forest. The thrashing and stomping sound stopped and seemed now to be going in the other direction.

Frank cautiously put the pistol back into the holster and slowly walked over to the trap. Everything became silent again. As he bent down onto his knee, he felt the large prints.

"These are fresh prints," he announced out loud.

As Frank trudged through the snow on his way home, he could see his log house in the distance. The door was wide open! Frank began to run toward his house. When he got there he quickly stepped inside the log house. There was flour all over and a trail of blood leading out the back door.

He slowly walked out the back door. He stood there looking at a half-eaten lynx carcass when he noticed it was missing one leg. There were large footprints leading away similar to the ones that he had seen earlier at the trap.

Frank quickly walked back inside and grabbed a trap, some poison, his .300 Winchester magnum, and a box of .300 magnum shells, then walked back outside. In a dense patch of trees, he saw a huge brown animal move. Frank quickly popped four shells into the magazine of the .300 Winchester magnum. When he looked up, the animal was gone.

Frank quickly put the lynx carcass into the trap and left, following the large footprints back into the forest. Bo followed close behind. As Frank walked farther into the forest, he could hear the singing and chirping sound of songbirds which filled the woodland and the trickling of a small brook in the distance.

A loud thrashing of snow-covered bushes filled the woods. Frank quickly looked around for the source of the thrashing. Then he saw a large figure hovering just above the juvenile fir tree and ferns.

Frank slowly lifted the .300 Winchester magnum to his shoulder. As he peered through the six-power scope he slowly squeezed the trigger. "BANG!" The shot echoed through the forest, but the large bear didn't even budge.

"Dang, I missed," Frank yelled.

As the large bear began to run away, the sound of thrashing filled the woodland again.

Frank began to walk again, but faster, following the large grizzly's footprints. He walked for about twenty minutes when he saw traces of fresh blood in the snow.

So I did hit him, Frank thought to himself

Frank looked down at his watch. It was nearly one o'clock. That meant that he had been tracking the grizzly for almost four hours, so he decided to head back to his home.

When Frank reached his home it was about five-thirty in the evening, and the sun had just gone down. Frank walked inside and began cleaning up the flour that the grizzly had spread all over his house.

A couple of hours later Frank heard a knock at the door. He slowly walked over to his window and looked out. In the dim light, Frank could see that it was his closest neighbor, Bob. Bob lived about a mile away. He was carrying a shotgun in one hand and his dog's leash in the other. Frank walked over to the door and quickly opened it.

"Hi ya, Bob," Frank said loudly as he dodged Bob's dog, Henry, who tore past him in search of Bo.

"Hi, Frank," Bob replied.

"How are you doing?" Frank asked.

"Not good," Bob replied, sounding angry.

"Why? What happened?" Frank asked.

"It's this dang grizzly. He broke into my house twice," Bob announced sounding annoyed. "He even stole three lynx and one bobcat from my trap."

"That scoundrel's been stealing my lynx, too. He broke into my house today and spread flour all over," Frank said in agreement.

"Well, I came to see if you had any flour that I could borrow, but I guess you don't," Bob replied disappointedly.

"Well, see you later, Bob," Frank said.

"Come here, Henry," Bob called into Frank's house, and his dog ran quickly out into the snow.

"Bye, Frank," Bob yelled, as he disappeared into the darkness.

Frank walked back inside and settled down in his bed and fell asleep.

Frank suddenly awoke to the sound of barking. He quickly looked at the glowing digital clock by his bedside. It was one o'clock in the morning. Frank then heard a loud "clank" of pans hitting together.

Frank quickly grabbed the .41 magnum from his bedside and snuck out of the room with the .41 magnum cocked.

He saw the large figure in the darkness. He aimed the pistol and squeezed the trigger. As the loud bang echoed through the house, the figure disappeared. Frank cautiously walked over to where he thought it had been standing. Frank didn't see anything, but he heard a snorting sound behind him. Frank slowly turned around.

The large grizzly had pried open a cupboard and was sniffing a large jar of peanut butter. The massive bear was only about seven feet away. Frank cautiously raised his pistol as the looming creature quickly turned and began walking toward Frank.

Frank cocked the pistol that he still held in his hand, but before he could react, the bear had lunged forward, knocking Frank onto his back.

Frank could smell the scent of decayed meat from when he had wounded the creature. The grizzly leaned forward and grabbed Frank by the shoulder and liter-ally threw him across the room. Frank rested against the wall, only about half conscious, as the grizzly with two long bounds was right in front of Frank again. The grizzly, without hesitation, jolted down and grabbed Frank by the neck.

"BANG!" The sound of a gunshot echoed in Frank's ear. The bear's grip loosened as he fell to his side, landing next to where Frank lay silently.

Frank slowly looked up and saw Bob standing in the doorway holding a smoking rifle.

Frank lay next to the body of the grizzly with a look of relief on his face. He could feel warm blood running down from his shoulder.

"Looks like you need to get to a hospital," Bob observed as he helped Frank get up.

Bob walked Frank outside. The wind whipped through the trees making Frank's face numb. Bob helped Frank out to Frank's truck with the keys in one hand and an armload of towels for Frank's wounds in the other. Bob quickly unlocked the door and helped

Frank into the truck. Frank's body ached. He felt a sharp stinging pain in his neck and shoulder.

Bob turned around and yelled, "Come on, Bo!" Bo ran outside and jumped into the back of the truck.

It was nearly a two-hour drive to the emergency room of the hospital in Palmer, Alaska. Frank spent almost an hour in the emergency room. He walked out with his arm in a sling.

"I got sixty-three stitches," Frank told Bob.

"Well, at least you're not dead," Bob said.

"Thanks for saving my life, Bob," Frank said. "Anyway, how did you know that grizzly was at my place?"

"I heard gun shots. It was a good thing I got over there in time," Bob answered.

The two neighbors started the long ride home. Everything was silent except the humming sound from the windshield wipers that moved back and forth, clearing the wet snow that hit the windshield. They finally reached Frank's home.

Bob asked, "Could I borrow your truck to get home? I'll bring it back in the morning around eleven?"

"Sure," Frank replied in agreement.

Derek J. Oberg
Grade 6
Carl Sandburg Elementary School
Kirkland, Washington

Derek has handled a number of elements in this story very well. He certainly sets up a convincing struggle. He speaks of guns with an authority that convinces me completely. He weaves description throughout the narration, too, bringing the world of the story alive.

"Everything was silent except the sound of crunching snow under the snowshoes of Frank Gifferd and the sound of his Alaskan malamute, Bo, panting behind." "The wind whipped through the trees making Frank's face numb." The "scent of decayed meat" from the wounded grizzly. And "Everything was silent except the humming sound from the windshield wipers that moved back and forth, clearing the wet snow that hit the windshield." We are never allowed to forget what a cold and distant and unforgiving land we are in.

Despite the intense activity, however, do you find yourself feeling with Frank? I don't. Though Frank's actions are well and believably presented, I never know what Frank, himself, is feeling, what the marauding grizzly means to him, or even why he chooses to fight it rather than run away.

Who is Frank? Why is he in Alaska to begin with? What is he trying to accomplish in that harsh wilderness? What does the loss of the lynx from his trap mean to him? Is it only a nuisance, a bit of money out of his pocket? Or is he on the edge of giving up this life and the empty trap is the last straw?

If we knew the answers to these questions, we would know what the death of the bear and Frank's rescue by his neighbor means to Frank. And knowing that, we would feel his dilemma with him.

So the first step in revising "Frank and the Grizzly" would be to write a character sketch of Frank. What kind of work did he do before he came to Alaska? Or is he a native Alaskan? Why is he living alone, trapping for fur? Does he hate human society? If so, why? Or perhaps he has some goal he is working toward . . . to earn enough money to marry the woman he loves, let's say, the woman he hopes is still waiting for him in some gentler climate. Or maybe Frank is in this harsh place in order to prove something to himself.

What does the powerful, old grizzly mean to Frank? Is the bear the opponent Frank must defeat in order to believe in himself again? Why does he need such a challenge? And when the bear almost kills him and it is his neighbor who guns the beast down, what is Frank left feeling? Why?

Derek has written an active and exciting story. But only when he finds answers to the above questions will the reader feel the excitement along with Frank. With these answers in mind, the story could be rewritten. In the new version, the action would rise out of Frank's thoughts, his needs, his goals for himself. When the bear died, we would feel his death, because Frank would feel it. And when Frank came back, wounded, to his empty cabin, a cabin that must have been nearly torn apart in his struggle with the grizzly, that moment would have meaning, too.

Would Frank feel victorious? Would he be defeated? If you want to try rewriting this story, the answers to these questions will be up to you.

Here is another fast-paced story in which the main character struggles to solve his problem. Archie is enthusiastic and determined . . . and funny. And we know what he is feeling. He's in love. The question is, as you read "Anything for Staci," do you feel with Archie? Or is he out there all by himself?

Anything for Staci

"Mom," Archie shouted. "Have you seen Brewster?"

"Archie..." Mrs. Minkelstein sounded out of breath from running upstairs. She took a deep breath before she asked, "Okay, Archie, which animal is missing this time?"

"Brewster, my garter snake," he answered.

Archie watched his mom cringe. He thought she had gotten used to all of his pets, but he guessed a snake was something that could take years to get used to.

"I have to get ready for work, and you have to get ready for school, so we can look for him when we get home. Okay?"

"Ugh!" shouted Mr. Minkelstein from the master bedroom down the hall. Mrs. Minkelstein sighed and leaned against the wall as Archie ran down the hall. He returned a few seconds later holding Brewster, who was desperately trying to get away. Archie ran into his room, grabbed his backpack, put away Brewster, and ran all the way to school.

When Archie got there he was already ten minutes late, and Ms. Laughlin was calling roll. "Minkelstein . . . Archibald Minkelstein are you here?"

"Yes, ma'am," Archie answered, wanting to sink into the floor. There were a few mutters of "What a nerd" and "He is the geek of the world," but as usual Archie ignored them.

Just then a gorgeous girl walked into the room.

Wow, Archie thought, *I'd love to bring her to the Valentine's Day dance!*

"Hi," the girl said brightly. "I'm Anastacia Malone. You can call me Staci." Everyone mumbled hello, except Archie. He was too amazed that she of all people would show up in his homeroom. He stood up to go talk to her, but noticed that she was talking to Angela Mills, one of the most popular girls in the seventh grade. He knew that Angela thought he was a nerd, so he decided not to go over there.

110

After a few minutes the bell rang and Archie ran outside into the hallway. He tripped over his feet and knocked over Erma's books.

"Sorry, Erma," Archie said, and he walked off leaving his best and only friend standing there with her books on the floor.

She picked them and ran after Archie, but he didn't notice. He was too busy thinking about Staci.

"Archie, what is it with you? You've never ignored me like that. I'm your best friend!"

"Sorry, Erma, but I've just had the most wonderful experience! Guess what happened?"

"You won the lottery. . . or Student of the Year . . . or you won the Nobel Peace Prize for science! That's what happened, didn't it?" Erma was shouting now, and everyone was looking at them strangely.

"No, I just met Staci Malone. She's perfect . . . gorgeous, graceful, smart. She's been here ten minutes, and she's already one of the most popular girls!"

Erma looked hurt and answered softly, "That's nice."

Archie lived the rest of the day in a daze. He had found out that Mr. Katzer, the principal, had given Staci the locker next to his and given Jerry Berg (nicknamed the Hulk) a locker on the other side of the school.

Just after the bell rang, Angela came running up to Staci's locker. "Can you come over after school today? I live on Quentin Drive," Archie overheard Angela ask.

"I would, but I have ballet tonight," Staci answered.

Angela looked interested. "Where do you take ballet?" she asked.

"I just enrolled in Jefferson Academy," Staci answered happily.

111

"Oh! I dance there, too! Level four, on Thursdays after school!" Angela exclaimed happily.

"I'm in level four, too, but I take it on Mondays!" Staci looked excited. Angela and Staci walked down the hall giggling all the way.

If I'm going to ask Staci to the dance, Archie thought, *I'd better get her to notice me*. Before Archie knew what he was doing, he had enrolled himself in the beginners' class at Jefferson Academy. He found a pair of old worn-out size eleven-and-a-half ballet shoes and a light pink shiny leotard. Half an hour later he was ready to dance.

The bright studio had mirrors on three walls and two wood rails running all the way across the other. He quickly identified the rails to be something called a *barre*, which all professional and non-professional dancers used to warm up on. (You never know what you can learn by reading the *B* encyclopedia cover to cover.) There were about six girls lined up along the barre stretching their already limber legs to the top rung.

A tall dark-haired woman with a French accent entered the room. "Class! Let us start with the five positions. First, second, third . . ." she shouted.

I can't believe I'm going through this for a girl, Archie thought.

"Okay, class, move away from the barre. Let's try an *arabesque*." She stood on one toe and extended her other leg gracefully.

Archie copied her, forgetting that his ballet shoes had no grips on the bottom to keep him from sliding. As soon as he lifted his back leg he fell, flat on his face.

The next day Archie went back to school with a Band-Aid on his nose and forehead, but determined to

112

show Staci his ballet. After eating a quick lunch of school-made spaghetti, Archie slipped into the boys' room and put on his leotard, tights, ballet shoes, and tutu. He then made his way to the middle of the cafeteria. He motioned for Erma to start the tape of classical music he had brought with him.

In a second he was dancing awkwardly to "Für Elise" and everyone had stopped eating and turned to watch Archie dance. There were snickers all around the room, and both Staci and Angela had stopped and stared on their way from the lunch line to the table. Embarrassed and tired, Archie ended the song with an arabesque. Not noticing how close Staci was standing, he sent her spaghetti flying. Staci screamed as the spaghetti flew onto her face and blue sweater and into her fluffy blonde hair.

Archie ran away as fast as he could in his no-grip shoes.

On Thursday, the day before the Valentine's Day dance, Archie slipped a Valentine into Staci's locker. It read:

> *My love for you is greater than the*
> *Great Wall of China.*
> *Meet me at 3:00 today, outside*
> *the school.*
> *With great love, Your Secret Admirer*

At three o'clock Archie went to the front of the school. There was Staci standing outside the school looking around.

"H-h-hi, S-s-staci . . . um . . . how are you?" Archie stuttered.

"Ah ha! I thought it would be you that sent me that Valentine!" Staci looked like she was going to laugh.

"How did you know?" Archie asked, confused.

The laughter Staci had been holding in exploded. "I've been compared to many things in my lifetime, but never to the Great Wall of China!" She went into another gale of laughter.

"Hey, it took me three hours to think of that metaphor!" Archie was steaming mad.

"Ooh, the nerd wants to fight?" Staci said with a sly smile.

This was too much for Archie. "I was going to take you to the dance, but you are such a snob I'm not going to!"

"I wouldn't have gone with you anyway, even if you asked me. Ta-ta, you nerd. Why don't you take Erma Urkel to the dance?" she shot back, and then trotted off to join Mark Zizmore and Kevin Schwartz.

At that moment Erma came running up beside him.

"Hey, Erma, do you want to be my date to the Valentine's Day dance?" Archie asked.

"Of course, but aren't you taking Staci?" she asked, suddenly sounding sad.

"No way, Erm. She's a snob, and she doesn't like me anyway."

"I'll meet you here at seven tomorrow night, okay?"

Erma looked happy now that Staci was out of Archie's life. Archie and Erma parted, and Archie walked home, sorry that he'd made a fool of himself, but happy to know what Staci thought of him. As he walked he knew that Erma was the right girl for him, because she respected him. He was going to have a great time at that dance.

Amy Webster
Grade 7
Osseo Junior High School
Osseo, Minnesota

Amy has not only created an active main character, she has also revealed Archie's feelings well. We know that he wants to "sink into the floor" when he is late for school, that he is instantly attracted to Staci, that he is afraid to approach her when she is talking to Angela Mills, who thinks he's a nerd. All of this connects us with Archie and draws us into his story.

Archie wants to take the popular new girl to the dance, and he sets out to do so. The things he does don't help, but that's all right, too. He embarrasses himself so thoroughly that by the end of the story we can believe in his change of heart. When he decides to take his faithful friend Erma rather than keep trying to be accepted by Staci, we are relieved. He doesn't need any further humiliation. And yet, though I know what Archie is feeling and even why he does the outrageous things he does, I don't find myself feeling with him. Why?

The steps Archie takes to try to get Staci's attention are funny. However, they are also rather difficult to accept. Though Archie is set up to be a likable "nerd," it's hard to imagine a boy so socially dense that he would try to attract a girl's attention by dancing a ballet in the school lunchroom. Especially after only one lesson. *Especially* dressed as a ballerina! And I find myself wondering why Erma still wants to go to the dance with him after he has made such a fool of himself over a girl who has never once glanced in his direction.

Humorous writing can be the most difficult to do successfully. The humor comes from stretching the truth, but for the stretch to work it must usually be based in solid psychological reality. We have to be able to believe that this character really would do such an outrageous or inappropriate or whimsical thing in such a situation. If we don't believe in the character's motivations and actions, we won't care about them either.

There is one aspect of Archie's life as it is presented here that I do believe in, and care about, too. That is his menagerie of animals. The first paragraphs, with Archie shouting "Have you seen Brewster?" and the whole family reacting, are both plausible and funny. I can believe in Brewster loose in Archie's parents' bedroom in a way I can't believe in Archie's dance in the lunchroom.

What if Archie used his animal collection to try to impress Staci rather than going off on the tangent of learning ballet? The author could set up an escalating series of events in which Archie approaches Staci with different strange animals. The culmination could be a general disaster in which one of them, perhaps Brewster, is loose in the classroom or lunchroom, and Staci, who predictably would *hate* snakes, would overreact. Using Brewster in the story would also give the opening a significance it doesn't have now.

I can even imagine faithful Erma being the one who helps Archie resolve the disaster in the end. Since they are best friends, she probably likes his snake. And when she helps out, Archie would suddenly see *her* in a new light. That would be a stronger conclusion than having him settle for Erma because Staci won't have him and because Staci, herself, told him he should ask Erma.

Beyond making Archie's actions more believable, though, another element is needed for me to fully feel Archie's plight. I need to understand why he falls in love with Staci. Surely he must know she is beyond him. After all, she is instantly the object of everyone's attention, and Archie knows that the other kids consider him "the geek of the world."

What, specifically, is there about Staci that makes him ignore everything he knows about his own possibilities? Her being beautiful isn't enough. There must be other beautiful girls in Archie's school. I would be far more apt to share his in-love state if I knew not just *what* Archie is feeling but *why* he is feeling it.

So, your main character must remain active, but the action needs to be understandable and believable and clearly felt. If the action is all those things, your readers will feel your story . . . which is precisely what they were hoping to do when they picked it up.

Another way of experiencing a story is by being caught up in its tension. And building tension is what we will discuss next.

CHAPTER 9

Building Tension

"I couldn't put it down!" We have all said that about a story we have loved reading. But what is the author's secret? How do writers, with nothing more exciting at their command than words, create stories that mesmerize us so completely?

The first answer that comes to mind is that a writer holds readers' attention with strong action. And that is sometimes the way it is done. In fact, the term "cliffhanger" speaks of a reader's being left "hanging" because of a character's very physical peril. But some totally absorbing stories actually have little physical action. And, as we saw in the previous chapter, physical action alone won't hold our attention.

Here is a very active story by a young writer:

Alone

I was about one thousand feet above ground and rising. I was still upset about having to go on this stupid parachuting trip with Dad, but Mom had made me. She said Dad had been looking forward to this for a long time, plus it was going to be "fun." Dad knew a friend from work who had a plane, and he was going to fly us.

I looked out the window at the mass of evergreens below us. We still had about fifteen more minutes until we'd be at Ross Lake where I would parachute down to the bank of the lake.

I was listening to the hum of the engines when suddenly the engines started to make a clanking noise! I looked out the window and saw one of the engines on fire! All of a sudden, the cabin started to shake, and the door broke open! Dad and I were thrown around the cabin.

Dad yelled out, "Kim, hold on!"

I caught onto a cabinet handle, but my hand slid off! The next thing I knew, I was falling out the door!

I began to panic. Fifteen is too young to die! Then I remembered the parachute. I groped around for the parachute release string. I found it quickly. I pulled the cord. The ground that was coming toward me at a fast rate started to come more slowly. The parachute had opened!

Slowly, I landed on the moss-covered ground. I was glad about being alive.

Suddenly, I thought about my father. I decided to put that thought out of my mind, because I knew in my heart he was okay.

I looked at my surroundings. All that I could see was dense forest. I gathered up my parachute, thinking that it would probably come in handy soon.

I immediately knew I was lost. There had been a strong wind when I had fallen, so I wasn't where Dad and the pilot thought I was.

It was already about three o'clock, so I decided to build some sort of shelter and then look for food. First, I picked up a large stone and started looking for some strong, sturdy branches. Once I had found the branches, I pounded them into the ground with the stone. After that, I ripped off part of the parachute to make a strange but well-built tent.

It had taken an hour to build the tent, so I decided to search for food. When I had landed I had heard the rushing water of a stream. It was north of where my tent was, so I headed in that direction.

After walking for about five minutes, I came to a rushing stream sparkling in the late-afternoon sunshine. It was about three feet wide. I walked downstream a little and came to a small pond full of trout and sunfish. Their scales shone in the sunlight.

I looked around and saw a long line of ivy that looked strong enough to hold a good-sized fish. Next, I needed a pole. I ran to the nearest tree and broke off a limb that was about three feet long. "Now all I need is a hook!" I said to myself. In frustration, I stuffed my hands into my pockets and found a sharp object. I pulled out a hook! It must have been from the fishing trip I had been on two days before. I fastened the hook onto the string of ivy, dug for worms, and started fishing.

By the time I started back to the camp, I had caught three good-sized fish, but I left one to float in the stream for breakfast. When I reached camp, it was already dusk, so I started to build a fire. After the fire was going, I cleaned the fish.

I cooked the fish over an open fire. I hadn't eaten lunch that day, so I ate both fish. I had brought some water from the stream to drink with the fish in an old bucket. I had found the bucket at the stream, and I had cleaned it out.

After I finished the fish and a fair amount of water (I still had some left in case I got thirsty), I felt sleepy. I used the rest of the parachute as a sleeping bag.

Since it was cold that night, I wanted to keep warm. I decided not to put out the fire, hoping it wouldn't go out in the middle of the night. I also didn't put the fire out, hoping it would attract any passing planes. Soon I fell asleep.

In the middle of the night I woke up smelling smoke. I rubbed my eyes and looked around. My "sleeping bag" was on fire! I quickly wiggled out and ran to the bucket of water. I ran back to the "sleeping bag" with the bucket of water and dumped it on the flames.

As soon as the fire was out, I sat down to think about what had just happened. "The sleeping bag must have edged its way over to the campfire," I said to myself. I looked at the campfire which was just about to go out and decided to go back to sleep, even though I could only use half of the "sleeping bag" since the other half was soaking wet. I had trouble getting to sleep because of the drenched "sleeping bag," but after a while, I drifted off to sleep again.

The next morning, after going to the stream to get more water and the other fish, I decided to build a fire to keep warm, to attract any passing planes, and to cook breakfast.

Except for a fishing excursion to get lunch and dinner, I just sat around feeling homesick and wondering what had happened to my dad.

That night after dinner, I was listening to the owls

when I heard what sounded like a big man coming through the bushes. I looked up. "Dad?"

Suddenly, I saw a large bear looking down at me, growling! For about ten seconds, I just sat there in shock. Then I thought about the fire! Animals are afraid of fire! I picked up a large burning branch from the fire and threw it at the bear. I knew all those years in baseball would pay off! The bear roared, turned, and ran back into the woods. I could hear the crashing of bushes for a long time. I hoped the bear was far away.

That night, I slept like a log. Early the next morning, I woke to the sound of voices. I peered out of the tent. There were two crude men who seemed to be planning something! Suddenly, one of the men turned, saw me, and yelled, "Look, there she is! Get her!"

I quickly picked up two small logs that by some stroke of luck were lying at my feet. I heaved them at the two men! The logs hit both men in the head and knocked them out. I was just about to go inspect the men when I heard gunshots. I looked up and saw a small line of smoke drifting into the sky. Hoping the smoke was coming from a house with a telephone, I began to run.

After running for about ten minutes, I came to a large meadow filled with the sounds of life. In the middle was a small but cozy-looking house. The house was white with green shutters and a red-shingled roof. The house had a red brick chimney and smoke was curling out of it. A man on the porch was shooting at game in the other direction.

When the man stopped to reload his gun, I ran up to him and told him my story. I asked him if he had a telephone, and if so, could I use it. He said, "Certainly."

I phoned my parents and was relieved to hear my father answer the phone. I told him I was okay. The man told my dad where he lived.

Ten minutes later, a helicopter landed and my parents jumped out. The first thing I said was, "Mom, you said this would be fun!"

When we were done hugging and kissing, we flew home. At home after a large lunch that included almost every food besides fish, I asked my father what had happened to the plane after I had fallen out. He said that as soon as I had fallen out, the pilot had called for help and reported the plane's position. He and the pilot parachuted from the plane, about a mile from where I had. Soon some men had come in a helicopter and picked them up.

That night as I was falling asleep, I thought about my adventure and decided to give up parachuting. But who knows? Maybe I'll take up mountain climbing or deep-sea diving. This adventure stuff is cool!

Sophie Calderon
Grade 6
Carl Sandburg Elementary School
Kirkland, Washington

In a note attached to her story, Sophie told me that she loves to write adventure stories, and this is certainly an adventure story. In fact, it would be difficult to imagine a story with more action. From the strong opening, "I was about one thousand feet above ground and rising," the action never stops. The main character falls out of a plane, parachutes to the ground, has to create her own shelter and find food, is attacked by a bear and later by two men, hears gunshots, and finally escapes to a place from which she can contact her parents, who come to bring her home.

The action is nonstop, and the main character certainly stays in charge of it. There are some good descriptive details, too. The description of the plane's engine going out and the narrator's being thrown out of the plane is a case in point. The moment when the narrator looks up and says, "Dad?" only to see a large bear is a good one, too.

However, on the whole there is more action in this story than there is tension. Why?

First, we are confronted with the same problem we discussed in the last chapter in connection with "Frank and the Grizzly." We don't know who this narrator is. She has no history. No individual traits, for that matter. We come to know nothing about her that would distinguish her from any other girl who happened to be thrown out of a plane. People care about individuals, not generic human beings. That is why, as I discussed earlier, character development is the most important single key to writing a good story. Readers care very little about characters they don't know.

If you were to revise Sophie's story, you would need to begin by answering some basic questions about the narrator. For instance, what does it mean to this girl to find herself suddenly on her own? Has she always thought herself brave, a real outdoorswoman, and now does she begin to question her own self-definition? Or is she the kind of girl who loves malls and public pools and hates to get her hair mussed? Is she going to change in the course of this adventure, or is she simply going to come through it without harm? A character who changes is always more interesting than one who doesn't. A character who changes can be more challenging to create, too.

By the ending she has chosen, Sophie has suggested a change. The narrator has gone on this expedition with her father only because her mother insisted that she do so. In the end, although she doesn't intend to go parachuting again, she is open to other adventures. But such a suggested change still leaves us with many questions. For instance, why did the girl's mother tell her she should go parachuting with her father? Why did her father want to take her when she didn't want to go? Most important of all, what happened inside the narrator during the adventure to bring about her change in attitude by the end?

Even if we knew the main character well, however, a problem remains that would reduce the story tension. As in "Anything for Staci," the logic of the events is strained. In this case there are too many coincidences. The girl just happens to have a fish hook in her pocket so that she can catch fish. She stumbles upon an old bucket in the stream. Two small logs "by some stroke of luck" are lying at her feet when the men accost her. And she is able to throw them both at once, knocking both men out instantly.

Coincidences certainly do happen in real life. We remark upon them all the time. In stories, however, the reader is always aware that there is a writer in charge of the events. Coincidences that work to the main character's benefit, as these do, are hard to accept. And story tension dies when the reader stops accepting the writer's premise. Thus a story filled with strong action won't necessarily generate high tension unless the writer makes the action believable.

Another technique, essential to building story tension, is the careful use of details. Important events need to be played out, using the main character's senses, thoughts, and feelings. The number of words devoted to a story event have little to do with how long it takes for the event to happen. The number of words used should have everything to do with how important an event is, how much attention the writer wants the reader to pay to it, how much tension the writer wants to build.

Note this brief example from the middle of another story, one involving a theft from an old woman.

Up in her room, Miss Douval was instantly awakened by the noise at the front door. Her curiosity could not be contained. Getting up, she put on her robe and walked down the stairs clutching the key to her safe which always hung from a chain around her neck. She was reassured when she felt the key to her wealth still around her neck.

Reaching the bottom of the stairs, she began to walk more quietly and fearfully toward the study where she heard voices whispering. Each step she took made her heart beat even faster. Reaching the study door, she curled her fingers around the knob and slowly and silently opened it a crack.

"Your phone seems to be dead. The storm must have blown it out," she heard a voice say.

Andrew Hand
Grade 9
Shenandoah Valley Academy
New Market, Virginia

Even without knowing the characters, even without knowing much about the situation, can you feel the tension here? It is created by the small but significant moments the author chooses to depict. When Miss Douval clutches the key to her safe and feels reassured, we are anything but reassured. Notice the effect of lines such as "Each step she took made her heart beat even faster. Reaching the study door, she curled her fingers around the knob and slowly and silently opened it a crack."

If every moment of a story were stretched like that, the reader would lose all patience after a page or two of reading. But when that kind of meticulous detail is saved for a high moment in the story, the reader is compelled to read on.

Go back to "Alone" and take one strong moment in the story, any one that appeals to you. Rewrite it, playing it out in the kind of detail Andrew has used in the brief paragraphs I have quoted. Can you make the tension build?

As I mentioned before, not all story tension is based upon physical peril. Sometimes the tension can be entirely psychological. Or, as in the next example, the tension may come from a mixture of the two.

What follows is part of a chapter from a long novel.

How I Became a Hero

[The story opens with our being introduced to Darwin, a puppy who thinks he is a cat. He gets into trouble with his family and is delivered to the pound.]

Chapter Four

Nicole's mother took me to the city pound. Not realizing what was happening, I yipped happily at the end of my leash.

But the pound . . . oh, the pound was such a dark, gray, scary place that I soon lost my happy skip and cowered along the cold cement floor.

Nicole's mother spoke to a tall man with hands that were cold when he picked me up by my collar and carried me off through a long dark hall lined with kennels of barking dogs. The man stopped beside a cage at the end of the hall. He opened the door and set me down on the hard floor.

"Here ya are, fella," he said, bending over to unbuckle my collar. "Won't be needing this anymore."

I looked at him curiously as he slammed the cage door and walked away.

"Wait! Stop! Come back! Where are you going? I have to go home with my people! Nicole and Milo will worry! Wait!" I pleaded, jumping up and leaning against the steel doors.

It was too late. The door at the end of the hallway slammed shut and left me alone in the pound cage. But I wasn't alone.

As I wept to myself, I heard the creaking of the doggy door fastened to the wall of the cage and a voice behind me saying, "Hey there, little one. What's wrong?"

I turned around and gasped in horror. This was the most horrible dog I'd ever seen. He loomed over me. He was tall and lean and his powerful muscles showed through his shiny black fur. As he stepped closer to me I backed away in fear.

"Oh, don't be afraid," he tried to say kindly, but when he opened his mouth, I could see his sharp, white pointed teeth.

"What's your name, little one?" he asked as I backed away further. The cage wall was blocking my way, and I was cornered. I did what Milo had taught me to do when confronted by a strange dog. I hissed at him. I hissed in his face and tried to scratch him on the nose.

This merely startled him, and he picked me up in his mouth and set me on the burlap cushion in the corner of the cage. Placing a large paw on my back so I couldn't move, he said, "Well now, little one, will you kindly tell me who you are?"

"My name is D . . . Darwin, sir. Please don't hurt me! Please!" I begged in answer.

"Hurt you? Hurt *you*? Why on earth would I do that?" he laughed.

"But you look so . . . so *mean*!" I explained.

"Mean? Me?" He looked at me in surprise. "My dear Darwin, Sebastian is only mean to one living animal in this world."

"What's that?" I had to ask.

"Cats. Sebastian is only mean to cats, of course," he said in a cold voice. "Only a cat could do this." He turned his head to reveal three deep pink scars on the side of his head that appeared to have been made by the claws of a cat. . . .

Laura Rogers
Grade 6
J. F. Luther Middle School
Fort Atkinson, Wisconsin

And the story moves on with the threat of Sebastian's discovering that Darwin is a "cat" always hovering, quite ominously, in the background.

Laura is especially successful in sustaining tension throughout her long story. What are some of the techniques she uses to keep the tension high?

First, Laura makes us like Darwin, her main character. And that liking, more than any other factor, keeps us reading the story. The puppy who thinks he is a cat has a sprightly and entertaining voice, a voice that makes him distinctive and appealing. And knowing and caring about Darwin, we are easily drawn into his story.

Second, Laura lets us know what Darwin is feeling so we can feel with him. "But the pound . . . oh, the pound was such a dark, gray, scary place that I soon lost my happy skip and cowered along the cold cement floor." She also lets us experience the world through Darwin's senses, which is another way of letting us share his feelings. "I turned around and gasped in horror. This was the most horrible dog I'd ever seen. He loomed over me. He was tall and lean and his powerful muscles showed through his shiny black fur. As he stepped closer to me I backed away in fear."

Third, Darwin's behavior is always believable, even for a puppy who thinks he is a cat.

And finally, Laura plays out crucial scenes in detail. Go back and reread Darwin's meeting with Sebastian and notice how the puppy's tension—and the reader's—is played out, moment by moment, to keep it high.

Story tension begins with a main character we care about and a story problem that is important to that character. The character's strong feelings about the

problem let us feel strongly, too. Story tension is sustained through believable action, action that fits the
character and does not rely on coincidence. And it is
sustained through careful pacing . . . summarizing or
passing over all that is unimportant, playing out crucial
moments in careful detail.

"I couldn't put it down!" What a fine thing to hear
readers say about a story! As you learn the techniques
for keeping story tension high, you'll be likely to hear
those words about one of yours.

Next, let's consider the impact and significance of
the ending you choose.

CHAPTER 10

The Meaning in the Ending

In the many years I have taught writing, I have seen hundreds, perhaps thousands, of fiction manuscripts from writers of all ages. And among all those manuscripts I have encountered many examples of fine writing.

I have discovered beginnings that pulled me into the stories and plots that held me, page after page. I have encountered descriptions that gave a story life and characters who seemed to have been born on the page. I have read conversations so genuine that I might have been eavesdropping on my neighbors and stories so tense that I have been compelled to read on. Despite all that, though, too often I have come to the end of an otherwise good story and been disappointed.

Why are endings so difficult to get right? To begin thinking about that question, let's look at a story in which the author does something unusual with the ending.

One Shot

The crowd was in an uproar as Jerome Gaines made his way to the free-throw line. His heart was racing, and his mind was moving even faster. It was the championship game, and Georgetown found itself tied with Arkansas with one second left. Jerome Gaines was in his senior season for Georgetown and had no idea what to do.

Two weeks earlier, only two days after Georgetown had beaten North Carolina to make it into the NCAA Championship, Jerome had been in the team workout room when two men approached him and asked if they could have a word with him. Jerome did not know who they were or what they wanted, but he followed them without giving the matter any thought.

When they got to an isolated part of the parking lot, they stopped. This was the first time Jerome could clearly get a good look at them. One was comparatively tall and well built. He had a look of intelligence. The other man was somewhat more portly with more hair on his face than his head.

The taller man turned toward Jerome and with a slight tone of arrogance in his voice asked him, "How would you like to make yourself a rich man?"

Jerome was pretty confused, but he was eager to listen, because at the moment he could use the money.

The man could see Jerome was not quite understanding what he was saying, so he went on. "You see, Jerome, I have got a lot of friends who have large sums of money riding on a certain championship game, and it's not on Georgetown."

Now Jerome knew what he was asking, and he was infuriated. To think that anybody would ask him to throw a game. He just could not believe it. He asked the man what in the world he thought he was, "A piece of meat or something?"

The chubby man calmly looked down the cigarette

he was dragging on and took a step toward Jerome and asked him if he would just consider it. With this comment, he handed Jerome his card and walked away.

That night Jerome was in his room watching television when the phone rang. He turned the TV off and walked over to the phone; it was his mom calling to wish him luck on the upcoming game. After he had finished talking to his mom, he sat back on his couch. All he could think about was his mom. She had never had a thing, and he had always wanted to give her everything. She had worked so hard to put food on the table and clothes on his back. He couldn't bear to think about it anymore, and turned the TV back on.

That night he could not sleep. All he could do was think about the offer. He couldn't believe he was even entertaining the offer. He couldn't go against his team. They were his friends and were counting on him. Then he thought of his mom again and how he could get her out of the ghetto with the money he would get from this. He wondered what would happen if he did not make the NBA, how would he take care of his mom then? He couldn't do much with his degree in communications because he never went to class enough to learn how to use a telephone, much less get a job.

When he woke up the next morning, he knew what he had to do. He picked the card up from the table and dialed the number that was on it. He recognized the voice of the man who answered the phone. It was the tall, sophisticated-looking one. Jerome asked him what he had to do. The man told him he just had to shave a few points off the score, just enough to let Arkansas squeak by. The man told him if he did that, he would be a hundred thousand dollars richer.

134

When Jerome got off the phone, he had a sick feeling in his stomach, but he couldn't think about it. He just couldn't.

The next two weeks were agony for Jerome. He couldn't shake that feeling in the pit of his stomach. He wished the game would come so he could get the inevitable over with. He never thought it would be this bad.

The game finally came, and as Jerome walked out onto the court, he knew what he had to do. Jerome only had two points the first quarter, but he had four turnovers. Despite Jerome's bad play, Georgetown was up through the second half. The game was tied when Jerome was fouled and sent to the line with one second left.

The crowd erupted in a screaming frenzy as Jerome stood at the line. He looked at his teammates. How could he let them down?

His eyes turned to the crowd. There he noticed a tall, well-dressed man staring coldly at him. He stared directly at the rim, spread his fingers on the ball, and shot.

Nathan David Hunt
Grade 9
Shenandoah Valley Academy
New Market, Virginia

What is your reaction to the ending Nathan has given you? Are you intrigued, ready to move into the story and decide on the ending for yourself? Or are you annoyed? Do you feel cheated because the author has withheld the main character's decision? What meaning does the story have for you?

Nathan's story provides an excellent opportunity for weighing the impact of story endings. Everything he intentionally withholds is what an ending is meant to provide: A sense of closure. Some important revelation about the main character. (Does he get what he wants? What does he want, finally?) And most important, the story's significance. By not giving us Jerome's decision at that final moment, Nathan chooses not to give his story meaning.

Reading a story in which the ending is withheld can be an exercise in frustration. It can also be a doorway to thoughtful discussion. Though I have never written a story without an ending, as Nathan has here, I usually leave some important elements open. That way readers are forced, as we are in "One Shot," to carry the main character and his dilemma away with them when they finish reading. It is a way of seeing that my story goes on living in my readers' minds. However, I never begin to write a story without first knowing what ending I intend.

Writing a story without an ending in mind is usually a setup for failure. The writer's knowledge of the ending is what gives direction and weight to each moment along the way. Too many beginning writers embark on writing a story without any idea of where they intend to go . . . or what the ending will mean when they get there. No wonder they often get lost along the way.

A writer who knows the ending she intends can give significance to every story moment. The author of the next story, "The Best Birthday Present," clearly had her ending in mind from the first line. Read the story. Does the ending give the story meaning? Does the ending satisfy?

136

The Best Birthday Present

"How could you?" Taylor asked between sobs.

"Well, Taylor, I did have other things on my mind."

"Were they more important than your best friend's birthday?"

"No," I said, ashamed. "But I've told you over and over how sorry I am and how much your friendship means to me."

"Then why did you forget my birthday, Carrie Bamford?" Taylor sobbed.

"I don't know, Taylor. I keep asking myself that same question. I guess I forgot because I was so busy practicing for the school play. The play is only a week away, and you know I'm so nervous about playing the lead!"

Taylor was really mad. I could tell because she used my last name. Just then I heard the door slam. I looked around the room and I was the only one there. Taylor Hudson, my best friend in the whole world, had walked out without saying goodbye.

"Great, just great," I said to myself. I had forgotten my best friend's birthday, and to make it worse, my birthday was in six days. I was having my first ever boy-girl party. Taylor and I had spent months planning this "big event," but now because I'd forgotten about Taylor's birthday and had missed going to the mall with her to buy a super outfit to wear to my party all because of the play rehearsal, Taylor was furious.

I really didn't truly forget her birthday. I'd gotten her a gift and everything, but rehearsal had just gone on and on, and when I got to her house, she'd already left for the mall with her dad. But Taylor wouldn't let me explain.

I stormed up the stairs making as much noise as I could, went into my room, and slammed the door. I hated fighting with Taylor. She had enough troubles in her life without me adding more. Taylor's mother had died when her three-year-old sister was born. Her dad did the best he could, but he treated Taylor just like her little sister. Mr. Hudson was nice, but very strict. I guess he tried real hard to take the place of Taylor's mother.

"Maybe I should call her," I thought. I'm not supposed to use the phone when my parents aren't home, but what the heck, this was an emergency. I went downstairs, grabbed the phone, and dialed Taylor's number.

Mr. Hudson answered on the second ring.

"Hi, Mr. Hudson. Is Taylor there?" I asked in a rush.

"Well, hello to you, too, Carrie," Mr. Hudson said. "I'm sorry you missed our big birthday night at the mall. We had a great time."

"I'm sorry I missed it too, Mr. Hudson." (Boy, if he only knew how sorry I was!) "Could I please speak to Taylor?"

I heard Mr. Hudson yelling for Taylor and in a moment Taylor's voice came on the line. "Hello."

"Uh, hi, Taylor. It's me, Carrie," I managed to squeak out.

The silence on the other end lasted forever. Finally Taylor said, "Oh, it's my ex-best friend."

"Look, Taylor. I'm really sorry about the mix-up in plans. Can't we just forget it ever happened?" I pleaded.

138

"I'm sorry too, Carrie. I thought we were best friends, but a real best friend would never forget something as important as a birthday," Taylor said angrily.

I tried one more time. "But we are best friends," I said. "I've explained what happened over and over."

"Carrie," Taylor said in a very stern voice, "do you know the definition of stupid?"

"Taylor, please. We're in the fifth grade. I think I know the definition of stupid," I said with a slight giggle in my voice.

"Do you want to hear my definition, Carrie?" Taylor yelled.

"Not really!"

"Well, I'm going to tell you anyway," Taylor yelled louder. "It's YOU!"

The phone banged in my ear and Taylor was gone. I slammed down the phone too. I know what I did was wrong, but *me*, stupid? I don't think so!

Suddenly I heard the front door open.

"Hi," Mom's cheery voice greeted me.

"Hi," I said happily. (I know I wasn't happy, but I didn't like to burden my mom with problems the minute she walked in the door from work.)

"What do you want for supper?" she asked.

I answered, "I don't care."

My mom laughed and said, "I don't think we have any 'I don't care.'"

"Not now, Mom," I whined.

"Oh, honey, where's your sense of humor?" my mother asked.

"In outer space, I guess," I mumbled under my breath.

"Now, Carrie," my mother said with a puzzled look, "what's wrong with you?"

"Nothing is wrong with me!" I yelled in a sarcastic voice. "I just didn't laugh at your dumb joke."

My mom said in her oh-so-soft I-mean-business voice, "Carrie Nicole Bamford, don't get smart with me."

I found myself saying, "And what if I do?" before I thought.

"All right, young lady. Go to your room until you decide to behave!"

With tears in my eyes, I ran to my room. After I lay down on my bed, my mind drifted back to the past. I saw myself at the hospital where Taylor and I had first met. I was about seven and had come to the hospital with my mom and dad to visit my Aunt Lisa. I had escaped out of my aunt's room to hunt for a candy machine because I was starving. As I walked down the hallway, I saw another girl my age sitting on a bench sobbing. Never one to be shy, I had gone up to her and asked what was wrong. That's how I'd met Taylor.

Taylor's mother had problems when she had Taylor's little sister and had died the same day. Taylor and I sat for a long time on that bench and just talked. It was like we had known each other forever. Taylor cried a lot, and I just listened. We later talked about where we lived and where we would both go to school that year. We were both surprised to find out that Taylor had moved in on our block a month earlier, but with her mother being so sick, she hadn't had time to meet many people. We ended up going to look at her new little sister in the nursery and grew to be great friends over the summer. By the time we started third grade together in the fall, we were best friends.

"Carrie, Carrie. Earth to Carrie," my mom was saying.

"What, what?" I asked.

My mother entered my room and sat on my bed. "Supper's ready if your mood has improved," she said.

"I'm sorry for the way I acted," I said, giving my mom a hug. "It's been a bad day. I'll tell you about it later."

"Well, that's more like my Carrie," Mom replied, and we walked downstairs together.

As we ate, I told my mom about the mix-up with Taylor. My mother suggested talking to her in person, so as soon as I ate, I ran down the block to Taylor's house.

Normally, I just knocked and walked in, but for some reason I rang the doorbell. Taylor's little sister, Beth, opened the door and said, "Hi, Carrie, did you come to play with me?"

"Not right now, Bethie. I need to talk to Taylor. Will you go get her for me?" I asked nervously.

Beth ran down the hall yelling, "Taylor, Carrie is here!"

When Taylor saw it was me, she started to shut the door in my face. Man! Did that get me steamed. I turned around and ran home and went straight upstairs to my room. After much tossing and turning, I finally fell asleep.

The next morning at school the first few subjects went by fast, and soon it was time for recess. I ran to meet Taylor at our place by the swings.

"Please, can we be friends again, Taylor?" I pleaded.

Taylor only said, "No!" and stomped off.

Recess passed all too slowly without my best friend to talk to. Soon we were back inside and the rest of the day crept by.

For the next five days it was exactly the same. The

141

only thing that helped was practicing. That was the only time I didn't think about Taylor.

The day of my big party finally arrived. Even though I had been excited before, now all I wanted was for the party to be over. How could I have fun without my best friend? I had sent out the invitations before I'd missed Taylor's birthday, so Taylor had been invited. People started arriving, and I tried to be happy, but the only thing I really wanted for my birthday was having Taylor as my friend again.

When I was reaching for the first present to open, the doorbell rang. I opened the door, and there stood Taylor!

"Taylor!" I squealed. "You came. You really came!"

"Oh, Carrie," she said, "I've been so miserable! I finally realized that I hadn't been fair to you. I've always expected you to be there for me, and when you didn't show up to go shopping on my birthday, I was so hurt. I know you didn't mean to forget, but I was just too stubborn to admit it. Can you forgive me?"

"Only if you can truly forgive me," I said as I gave her a big hug.

With that out of the way, the party really began! I looked at Taylor and realized she was the best birthday present of all!

Jaclyn Nicole Shaw
Grade 5
Evers Park Elementary School
Denton, Texas

"The Best Birthday Present" is a sophisticated story. It stays focused on the problem throughout. Carrie and Taylor are both well-drawn characters. We even get a brief history of their relationship slipped in without slowing the forward movement of the story. The dialogue is realistic and the events of the story believable. The internals allow us to experience the story problem through Carrie. We participate in her struggle to get her best friend back. And the resolution, when it comes, is exactly what we want.

One problem here, however, is that tension doesn't escalate. The failure of each attempt to get Taylor back leaves Carrie in exactly the same place she was in before she tried. As we discussed in the last chapter, tension needs to increase as the story moves on. Each attempt on Carrie's part should push Taylor further away until Carrie finally changes or discovers what she needs to do to bring her friend back.

And then there is another issue. Despite the fact that the story ending is exactly what I want it to be, I am not satisfied when it comes. Why not? Because though Carrie has certainly struggled to bring Taylor around— we have been with her through four attempts—in the end, Taylor comes back of her own volition. The problem is resolved without Carrie's help.

For the ending to be satisfying, Carrie must solve her own problem. As the story stands, Taylor solves Carrie's problem for her by seeing the light and coming around without Carrie's having done anything to cause the change. When Taylor does that, she robs the main character both of power and of the possibility for meaningful change.

In most successful stories, the main character must learn something along the way. It is that learning, that change on the main character's part, that gives the story meaning. If Carrie has nothing to learn, no change to go through, then the story has little to say.

For Carrie to change, however, she would need to

start in a place from which change was needed. What if, for instance, she had refused to apologize or explain from the beginning, figuring that Taylor should understand how important the play is to her? Then Taylor would only come around when Carrie finally had the courage and the humility to see her own error.

Or what if Carrie had intentionally chosen to "forget" Taylor's birthday? Instead of meeting Taylor, she had gone off with a new friend, a popular girl who is suddenly paying attention to her because she has the lead in the play. What Carrie would learn then is that Taylor is more valuable to her than this new, more superficial friend.

Either of these possibilities would allow Carrie to learn a lesson and, in learning it, to change. When she came back to herself she could then be able to bring Taylor back, too. Perhaps once Carrie has realized how important Taylor is, there is something she could do to bring Taylor around. A surprise party to make up for the missed birthday? Maybe she could sacrifice going to a cast party in order to help Beth, Taylor's little sister. And Taylor, discovering what Carrie has done, would realize that she truly is a friend.

The changes I have suggested, while they would give Carrie's struggle meaning, may not represent the story Jaclyn wants to write. Before Jaclyn could revise "The Best Birthday Present" she would need to decide what meaning the story has for her. When she knew that, she would know how Carrie needs to change. And in knowing how Carrie needs to change, Jaclyn could easily discover what course of action Carrie would need to take to win Taylor over again. Thus the entire plot would come out of the author's understanding of what the story means to her.

Here is another story. What meaning does this ending give us?

Future House

"Well? What do you think?" asked the realtor, grinning.

I looked up at the huge house. The outside looked like a mix between an observatory and your everyday, run-of-the-mill mansion. The dome was huge, with glass panels adorning its structure. They were not like windows, but more like mirrors, and the sharp reflection of the sun glazed down onto the ground, annoying my eyes. The rest of the outer structure looked like one of those twentieth century mansions that I would have killed to get back in 1996 (before I used a time machine I had built to transport myself to the year 2050). If only it hadn't broken. Everybody, for some reason, has found me a celebrity here.

I answered, "I wouldn't know. I haven't gone inside yet. Say, what's that dome up there for, anyway?"

"Well, nowadays, everything is solar powered!" the salesman supplied cheerfully.

"Hey! That's pretty cool! But what if it's nighttime?" I said, throwing that last comment in as a joke.

"No problem! In this particular model, solar power can be used even at night! It's not like we got rid of electricity completely!" he told me.

Good heavens, he's taking this seriously! I thought in horror as he opened up a small panel in the frame of the door and pressed a button. A huge lamp then popped out from the back of the house and shone down on the dome. He pressed it again and the lamp withdrew back behind the house.

"I hate to break it to you, but solar power works at night, too," I informed him.

"It does? Oh dear, *that's* why the architect got that letter from the National Scientific Foundation he tore up," he sighed. Then he perked up again, continuing, "This house also comes with a super duper security system!"

Having said that, he took out a robot about five feet tall called "The Incomputer" from his briefcase. (Okay, it was a laptop model.) He opened the robot's chest and entered a command. It zoomed to the door, trying to enter a code in the door lock system panel on the front door, which had every number from one through nine in it. I assumed that the robot was supposed to enter a wrong code in the system (hence the name, "The Incomputer"), because all of a sudden, a laser gun popped out from the upper left-hand corner of the doorway and zapped the robot to ashes. Then the system identified the robot in a calm, feminine voice and played "Taps."

"How's that? Bet you didn't have anything like this back in 1996," he gloated as he nudged me with his elbow.

"Well . . . it's . . . er . . . nice, and true, there was nothing quite like this in my time . . . ," I managed to say, trying not to hurt the man's feelings.

"Go on," he prompted.

"But shouldn't the computer identify the person *before* it zaps him or her? Then at least I get a chance to decide whether or not I want the person to be zapped," I finished.

"So that's why the last person who lived here left so abruptly. I was wondering why there were ashes in the front the day he disappeared," the salesman mused.

This isn't encouraging, I thought.

"Well, let's go inside, shall we?" the man suggested.

"Uh, I guess," I answered. Truthfully speaking, I was really dreading what might be inside.

Our first (and only) stop was the kitchen. "In today's world, food is dehydrated and put inside a small dissolvable capsule for easy transportation!" the realtor declared. From watching cartoons, I had sort of figured on that. He then led me to a huge machine and pressed a button with a tiny picture of a steak on it. Out popped a small red and white pill. The salesman pulled out a pre-filled eyedropper.

"Allow me to demonstrate the handy-dandy food pill. I must warn you never to put more than one drop of water on this."

Disaster approaches, I predicted.

"This steak is the best you've ever tasted. Why, if anyone else even claims to have a better steak, why I'd . . ." He tightened his fist, the knuckles turning white. Unfortunately, he had squeezed the hand with the eyedropper in it, and as a result, all the water fell out . . .

. . . onto the pill!

We blinked at each other for a second, then ran out the door of the kitchen. When we turned around again, the lower half of the kitchen bulged with steak and the upper half was filled with little food capsules because the steak had pressed all of the buttons of the food-pill dispenser.

"Well, now you know why you should never put more than one drop of water onto a food capsule. Don't worry. I'll call 911 after we finish exploring the house," he told me.

"No way! I'm outta here!" I shouted, running toward the door.

"Wait! Don't you want to see the V.R. machine? Or the smell-o-vision? Or . . ."

"I'd rather not," I shouted from the entrance.

"Don't you even want to see the time machine?" the realtor shouted desperately.

I stopped. "Time machine?" I mused softly.

"Yes! Ever since you created it, it's gone into mass production!" he said with new hope. "Come and see!"

I went into the room where he was standing. Sure enough, there it was, sitting on a desk. "Neat, huh? That's why everybody recognized you!"

"Say, can I take it for a spin? Just to see if it works like mine?" I asked.

"Sure! Be my guest!"

So I turned it on, set the coordinates, and pressed the GO button. And suddenly, I appeared about five minutes before I used the time machine I made on November 17, 1996. (Despite popular belief, when you use a time machine to go back to a time when you are still alive, you don't meet yourself. You become yourself in that time.) It must have been a first-year, unused model. It broke as soon as I used it.

Just as I had expected, my sister, Amy, came into my room. "Hey, is that your time machine, Beth?" she asked.

"Duh," I retorted.

"Say, now that you've created it, do you think people from the future could come and meet us?"

Before I would have told her that I was going to see for myself and would have used it. This time I thought for a minute. "Good point."

I ran to the garage, got the hammer out of Dad's toolbox, went back into my room, and smashed the time machine to pieces.

148

"Hey, what are you doing? Didn't you see the future? If you did, what was it like?" Amy questioned me.

"Frankly, Amy, you *don't* want to know."

Beth Badger
Grade 6
Ridgeway Elementary School
Renton, Washington

Beth has used humor very well here. The idea of a society in the future in which technology is both more intricate and more incompetent than what we know is amusing. And the main character goes through a change that gives the story significance. Presumably she starts out believing in technology and in the superiority of the future. Why else would she build a time machine and travel to it? By the end, however, she has lost all faith in the wisdom of the future and, in fact, destroys her time machine. It is a simple story and a simple change, but effective.

I find it interesting that this story is successful even though the main character is essentially passive throughout. Beth simply witnesses the various demonstrations of the new technology and takes note of how poorly they work. She doesn't take charge until she gets in the time machine and escapes back to her own time . . . and then makes the decision to destroy the machine so it can never be used again. Despite the lack of struggle in this story, the main character's taking charge and acting to bring about the ending gives the story significance and leaves the reader feeling satisfied.

Stories don't exist merely to move a character through a series of complications and see her emerge

149

with her problem resolved. They should mean something. Stories that are written with thought and care will reveal an author's deepest convictions. If we ourselves are without convictions, however, the stories we write will reveal our confusions. Perhaps that, more than any other factor, is what makes fiction difficult to write . . . especially when you're young.

How clearly I remember being young and wanting, quite desperately, to have *opinions* . . . about anything at all. The stories I told inside my head were rich and intense and complex, but I never wrote them down, because they had no endings . . . no meaning. I had no idea then why my stories obsessed me so. I understand now that they were part of my own search for meaning. It wasn't until much later, though, when I began to understand my own convictions, that I began to be able to create stories that had endings.

And yet it is possible, even for young writers, to know what they want to say. "The Best Birthday Present," for instance, is based on a clear conviction— that friendship is important, more important than having the lead in the school play or one's first boy-girl party. Once a writer has understood what she wants to say, the process of finding the ending to a story is not so hard.

To satisfy the reader, the character needs to bring about the resolution herself. The most interesting and believable solutions lie within our characters. If we know who our characters are, then we will know how they need to change. We spend our lives learning and changing. To be interesting, our characters need to learn and change, too.

A story without an ending has little reason to exist. A story with an ending that doesn't reveal something important about the main character fails to satisfy. Put your main character, a character you know and understand, in charge of working out the solution to his own problem, and your meaning will follow . . . and with it, reader satisfaction.

From the beginning of this workshop, we have been talking about revising. I have suggested, often, that you take someone else's story and revise. Finally, let's look more closely at the whole issue of revision. It is the point of a workshop, after all, to learn how to revise.

CHAPTER 11

Learning to Revise

Good writing happens in layers. This is true for professional writers as well as for beginners. The more complex the form we are attempting, the more layers we will need to discover before our piece assumes its final shape. Fiction writing is one of the most complex forms of all, so most stories must be revised many times before they attain their best form.

Writers setting out to tell a story they care about will find themselves, almost automatically, doing some things well. Perhaps your strength is believable-sounding dialogue. Maybe you love writing vivid description. Or you create characters who spring to life on the page. But despite the aspects of story writing you do easily and well, you will find yourself challenged, too. Every writer does. The first and most important challenge is to learn to identify ways you can improve the story you have written.

Never think of revising as fixing something that is wrong. That starts you off in a negative frame of mind: "I messed up. I have to do it again." Rather, think of it as taking an opportunity to improve something you already love. And it is the rare story that doesn't come into the world needing improvement. I know mine certainly do.

The problem, though, is that before you can make your story better, you must know what improvements are possible. Naturally you tried to do the best you could the first time through. What is needed when you return to your story is a re-vision, a new vision that will enable you to get a fresh perspective.

Do some aspects of your plot need to be rethought? Should you work out more about your characters' histories? Have you used your main character's senses, her thoughts and feelings, to enter fully into your story? Will your ending satisfy the reader?

The best way I know to begin to answer these questions is through a process of workshopping. Present your story to other writers for comments. What do they think works well? What can be improved? You will learn as much by helping others define where their stories need work as you will in hearing comments about your own.

I have set up a workshopping process for each of the stories presented in this book. First I talked about the story's strengths. Then I suggested the kinds of revisions that could make it stronger. Every newly written story deserves to be evaluated in that exact way.

If you find another writer—or several others—to join you in a workshop, use this pattern as a foundation for your discussions. Always consider a story's strengths before offering suggestions for improvements. It is easy to pick even the best stories apart. Defining strengths requires more thought and understanding.

Furthermore, never tell another writer—and never let another writer tell you—*how* to revise a story. Only point out the ways in which a piece might be strengthened and let the writer find his own way back inside the work to revise. If you start rethinking the story for the author, you will steal the creative energy he needs to see his story anew.

You might begin to develop your workshopping process by reading and discussing a story from this book. Here is a particularly effective one, which could nonetheless profit from being revised.

Rose's War

The rain pattered softly on Rose's head as she ran swiftly through the streets of Winnersburg. There weren't many people about since it was suppertime and everyone had gone in for the meal. Rose was running an errand for the cook. Mrs. Samual was baking bread for supper but had run out of flour. She had asked Rose to run to the mill for a sack of flour. That had been well over an hour ago, for Rose had stopped to pet the lovely nut-brown horse in the miller's pasture. She had secretly named him Chestnut because of his rich brown color. He was a beautiful horse with long legs and a smooth, silky coat. When he ran you could see his muscles rippling with strength. He was a horse to dream about, Rose thought.

As Rose stepped into the kitchen, warm aromas wrapped around her like a blanket: chicken, peas, mashed potatoes, and pie.

"Rose, there you are! Your mama is gonna be mighty mad at me for not making the bread for your supper! Go quickly and get your papa! Scoot!" scolded Mrs. Samual lightly.

Rose quickly ran out into the night with only a meek apology. In the barn William Winters was carrying a big bale of hay for Bill and Joe, the horses that pulled the Winterses' buggy.

"Father, you must come. The supper is ready."

"Thank you, Rose. I'll be there in a heartbeat," William answered kindly.

"Father, I was wondering. Have you heard any more news on the war?"

"No, sweetheart, but they are still fighting."

That night Rose thought about all of the news they had learned that week. It was hard news. For now the colony was in the middle of the Revolutionary War. Rose's parents were Tories, meaning that they supported the King. Many people Rose knew were Patriots and they wanted freedom. Rose never knew what to believe. She knew that she was supposed to believe in what her parents believed in, but sometimes to her that didn't seem right. Rose secretly believed that the Patriots were right.

Sometimes the news confused Rose, and it often got jumbled up in her head. It was hard for her. There also was the worry of Father going off to fight. That was a thought that Rose couldn't stand.

Her father was tall with snappy green eyes and sandy blond hair. Rose resembled him with the same eyes and hair. The only difference was personality. William Winters was a serene person and always calmed everyone down and kept everything together. Rose was wild and often caused the troubles in the family with her misdemeanors.

Rose's mother was also very kind, though she could be strict and very firm. Rose knew that on the inside she was a very thoughtful person and wanted the best for her family. Sometimes Patty Winters was very strict with Rose, because she wanted Rose to grow up to be a fine and proper young lady. When Rose did unladylike things, she lost her temper. Rose loved both of her parents and wanted the best for them.

That night Rose's dreams were of her riding off on Chestnut to fight so that her country would have freedom.

The next day, Rose's mother made Rose sew a dress for her younger sister, Elizabeth. As she sewed, Rose pricked her fingers ten times, and she was about ready to give up. Then when she was sewing on the sleeves, she found that she had cut the fabric wrong. *What a day*, thought a frustrated Rose as she ripped out all of her stitches. *I've already spent three hours inside, and I'm going crazy.*

Rose looked outside at Winnersburg's main street. She envied all of the people out there. The sky was bursting with fresh sunshine, and the air looked crisp. Rose could almost feel the people bustling around her and smell the candy and saddle grease at her father's general store. It was a lovely Massachusetts day, and the trees were lost in brilliant colors, reds, maroons, marmalade, gold, and brown. The leaves fell and danced on the ground, like ballerinas. As Rose looked around the stuffy and dim parlor, she longed to run outside even more. Rose swiftly looked around her. The house was silent, so Rose tiptoed out of the parlor and out the back door.

The air felt wonderful, though nippy, for Rose was without her cloak. She ran swiftly through the village until a sight made her stop short. Ahead of her there was a town picnic. There were many people and lots of food. The air wafted smells such as roast chicken, muffins and, best of all, ice cream! The Winterses had made ice cream on a few special occasions, and each time Rose savored every bite.

But as Rose turned, ahead of her there was an even better sight. There were races galore. There were three-legged races, sack races, running races, and many more that Rose didn't know. As she looked around, she didn't see any girls lined up to race. She saw many girls tending to their siblings and serving food, but none having any fun. That was when she decided that she would enter every race and try to win at least three. And she did.

Rose had the time of her life. There was no mother reprimanding her to be quiet or no evil task of sewing. She could run and whoop with joy. For the three-legged race, Rose ran to the picnic site and dragged back a girl named Lucy for her partner. Lucy was a quiet girl, and for some reason, she seemed surprised that Rose was there. This didn't bother Rose because she was busy explaining all the rules.

By dusk Rose was worn out. As she walked wearily along the cobblestone road she thought of her mother and father. Telling by her stomach, she figured she had been gone at least three hours. Rose knew that she was in for trouble.

"Rose Kathrine Winters, where in the world have you been? We have been worried sick about you! Were you out riding again?" Mrs. Winters practically spit out the words.

"No, Mother, I was . . ."

"Where were you?"

"I was at the town picnic. There were races and food and ice . . . ," Rose replied dreamily.

"You went to the town celebration picnic for the

Patriots! They were celebrating one of the battle victories. How dare you disobey me and go there! Well, young lady, I am sure you have had enough partying for one day. Up to your room. Go!" said Patty Winters in a horrified tone.

"But Mother I didn't . . . ," faltered Rose.

"Don't talk back, young lady. Go!"

As Rose lay in her soft bed, she could hear her parents fighting. She thought it was about her. Father wasn't there when Patty Winters made her little speech. Rose was sure that her mother was explaining what had happened. Now the voices were quieter, and Rose knew that they were talking about the war. They did a lot of whispering at night these days, just as Rose did a lot of thinking at night.

The next day Rose's mother asked her to go to the store and get her some embroidery thread. Rose happily agreed and skipped off to her father's store.

"Well, my young lady, may I offer my assistance?" said William Winters, grinning.

"Papa!" Rose replied, laughing. "Yes, Mother needs blue and yellow embroidery thread."

"Coming right up. By the way, Rose. There is a young girl about your age who was asking about you. Lucy Porter was her name."

"I know Lucy, Papa. Where is she?"

"With her father. I think where the flour is," William replied as he backed into the storeroom.

Rose slowly meandered over to the dry goods part of the store. Sure enough, there was a young, pale girl with shocking red hair. She was small and thin, resembling the man who stood next to her. Rose guessed that the man was her father.

"Lucy, good day. How are you?" said Rose in her usual loud and energetic fashion.

"I am fine, and you?" replied Lucy in a very quiet tone, as if she were whispering.

"I am doing quite well, thank you, except I got in trouble last night for going to that picnic. You know, the one in the park."

"You did?" said Lucy, looking very surprised, as if she were realizing something for the first time. "Why? Aren't you a Patriot?"

When Rose replied, "No," Lucy got very pale, but she soon regained her composure and requested that Rose join her and her family for hot chocolate.

"Well, Lucy, I don't know. I would have to ask my mother and father. First, however, I have to go home and give my mother her embroidery thread." Rose glanced toward her father who was standing at the table holding the thread.

"Well, how about we meet in the park tomorrow at noon. Would your mother approve?" Lucy questioned.

"Sure!" Rose answered as she ran to her father's table. "See you then."

That night at the dinner table, Rose told her mother and father that she would be meeting a friend in the park the next day at noon. She didn't say anything about meeting Lucy at the Patriots' Picnic or how Lucy said that they would have hot chocolate instead of tea. Rose figured that they were boycotting tea. Many of the Patriots were doing that since the Boston Tea Party. Rose knew that if she revealed any of that information to her parents she and Lucy would be unable to become friends.

The next day she and Lucy met as planned. Rose's

mother thought that she had finally met some nice young girl who might teach Rose some manners. That day Lucy and Rose had a wonderful time. They took a walk in the woods behind Lucy's house. The trees were alive, and Rose had never felt so free. They were so busy talking they didn't realize how long they had walked until they came to a clearing in the woods. There were bees and birds everywhere, and the air was quite warm for a day in late September. There were wild flowers all around and Rose made a bouquet in hopes of warming her mother's heart. As they walked on, they came to a brook and stuck their toes into the freezing water.

Soon Rose realized that it was very late, for the sky was darkening. Rose knew that she must get home quickly or she would be punished. They ran swiftly through the woods and got home in less than a half of an hour. Soon Rose was bursting through the door of her own kitchen with a fist full of small purple flowers. Rose was startled by the silence of her home.

"Mother, Father," Rose called in vain. Soon she heard a small voice coming from behind her. She turned and was face to face with Elizabeth.

Elizabeth's eyes were mournful as she told Rose that their parents were up in their bedroom. Rose knew that something was wrong, and she knew that she wouldn't get anything from Elizabeth. She ran speedily up the stairs and right into her parents' bedroom. The sight ahead of her made her stop short. Her mother was crying. *Her* mother was crying! Rose could not believe her eyes. She knew that if her mother was that upset, the news must be bad, very bad. Mrs. Winters rarely cried in front of her children. She was the kind of person who kept her thoughts to herself. Rose only remembered her crying once, when her brother, William Peter Winters Jr., died with pneumonia. Rose was only four and Elizabeth wasn't even alive. That memory had stuck with Rose for a long time.

"Mama, Mama, what is the matter?" Rose questioned worriedly.

It was William who replied. "Rose, I am going to have to join the British army. They are losing men, and they need me. I must protect the King."

And with that, Patty Winters let loose another uncontrollable sob.

Rose asked many questions and then fell silent. Rose couldn't imagine living in this house without Papa. Papa was the one who would resolve her arguments with Mama and who would keep her smiling when she had to serve tea and sew for her mother. Rose couldn't imagine life without Papa.

That night Rose cried herself to sleep.

The day that Papa was going to leave came all too soon. He had packed a bag with clothes, his rifle, and food that Mrs. Samual had prepared for the occasion. It was a sad departure for the Winters family, and there were many tears.

When it was Rose's turn to say goodbye, he spoke in a very soft tone. "Rose, you are in charge of the house now. You are the oldest, and I want you to keep things together for me. I also want you to obey your mother. She is worn out, and don't you go make it worse for her. You must stay loyal to your family. We need you. Now that I am making you in charge of your family, you will have more responsibility. You must watch your sister and help Mama with whatever she needs done.

Do you understand me? You are a young lady now. You are thirteen years old. I know I can count on you." And with that William Winters gave Rose a big hug and kiss, waved goodbye, and rode away with tears in his eyes.

Only then did Rose cry. She hadn't let herself cry ever since that night that seemed so long ago when she found out the awful news. She cried as she walked into the house and as she trudged up the stairs to her room. Her mother didn't even try to console her, knowing that it would do no good. Only when Rose was in her own room did she stop. It seemed as if all of her insides were dried up in misery.

In the weeks to come, Rose did her best to follow her father's wishes. She helped Mrs. Samual cook. She tended to Elizabeth and helped her mother in more ways than one. After a while Rose was going crazy. She had done so many chores, and it seemed as if she had been inside forever. Finally Mrs. Winters noticed and said, kindly, that each day Rose was to have the afternoon to do whatever she pleased (as long as she didn't get into trouble!).

Rose and her mother were getting along very well. Rose didn't get into trouble as much, so therefore Mrs. Winters didn't get angry. Rose knew exactly what she would do on her afternoon playtime. The very next day she met up with Lucy and they played and played. They went to the woods. They made paper dolls, and they also played with Lucy's brother.

Lucy's brother's name was Mike. He was tall and thin with the same red hair as Lucy. He was nice to Rose, and she liked him right away. Mike liked to talk about the war. Like his father, he was a Patriot, and

both of them were going to have to fight soon. Lucy was worried about what would happen to them and often talked about it. When Lucy talked like that, Rose got worried. Where was Papa? What was happening to him?

At night, Rose lay in her bed and she wondered where he was at that very moment. Did he have a warm bed to sleep in? Was he lonely for his family? Was he starving? Whenever Rose thought these terrible thoughts, shivers ran down her spine. It was very scary. There was one stubborn thought that kept coming into Rose's imagination. *What if Father gets killed by this dumb war?* She would always push it away, thinking of happy times she and her father had together with her family. They had gone on lovely picnics with just the four of them. They would play games and laugh and sing. They had never had all of that fun since the war started. It seemed to Rose that the war had wrecked everything. Rose often fell asleep with tears on her pillow.

In the next few weeks, Rose and Lucy became better and better friends. They played at Lucy's home and at Rose's. One day, Rose was teaching Lucy how to ride the Parkers' brown horse named Sam. Lucy had asked Rose to teach her so she could show her brother on his birthday as a surprise. Rose thought that Lucy was doing very well considering that she was scared to death of the big animals. Rose and Lucy had to have their lessons in secret because Lucy said that her mother and father didn't think that girls should ride horses bareback. Today, Lucy said that her father was off doing some business and her mother was in the parlor serving tea to Mrs. Winters and Mrs. Cotkins.

Rose and Lucy had the whole pasture to themselves.

"Good going, Lucy! You look grand on that high horse with your lovely locks swaying out behind you," said Rose, laughing. Actually, Lucy looked like there was a ghost behind her, and her hair was all tangled.

"Aye, I'm sure!" retorted Lucy.

Rose was having the time of her life. She felt almost completely happy, just as if there wasn't that lonesome nagging in her heart for Papa.

"Lucy, where are you dear? Rose, your mother and sister are ready to go."

"Uh oh! What if Mother finds me on this horse. Help, HELP me!" called a panicked Lucy as the horse ran faster and faster around the pasture.

"Rose, Lucy. Now where could they be?" called Mrs. Parker.

"Lucy, you are just going to have to jump. Otherwise it will be too late and your mother will find us. Don't fall!" cried Rose, but her warning came too late. Lucy slipped sideways off the horse and landed in a big, brown mud puddle.

"Dear me! Oh, there you are, dear Rose. Could you please tell the whereabouts of my daughter?" crooned Matilda Parker.

"Ah, well . . . ," stumbled Rose.

"Oh my stars! Lands sake, child. Why in the world are you in that mud puddle?" said a surprised Matilda Parker. "Oh no. Were you riding bareback after I told you not to?"

"Well, yes . . . but . . . ," stuttered Lucy.

"Up to your room. You will be punished! And Rose, your mother told me to tell you that she will see you at home. Now, if you please, could you gather your things and exit by the front door," said Mrs. Parker huffily as she picked up her long skirts and waddled back to the house.

"Yes, ma'am," whispered Rose underneath her breath. She then quickly ran up the back steps into Lucy's room. Lucy was nowhere in sight, so Rose quickly grabbed her sweater and left. On her way down the stairs, Rose heard some hushed voices in the Parkers' parlor. She recognized only two of the voices, Mike's and Mr. Parker's. There were many more people, and as Rose peered into the room, she saw many men dressed in the Patriots' uniforms. They were discussing something that seemed very serious.

Rose knew that she shouldn't be there, but she didn't know what would happen if she was seen, because to get to the front door she would have to walk through all of the men. Rose stayed silent and listened to what the men were saying.

"Well, we must win this battle. We must!" said a big burly man with a big white wig on. "We must devise a plan that will provide us with victory!" And with that he slammed down his fist on the antique mahogany table.

Rose sat on the steps and listened to what the men were saying. She found out some very important information. Supposedly, all of the Patriot soldiers were going to hide on the Tories' side of the battlefield. When the Tories were ready to fight, all of the Patriots were going to jump out and shoot them from behind. Rose soon left by way of the back door, because it looked as though the meeting was going to last a long time.

When Rose got outside, she breathed in the fresh air. She was shocked and also proud. Rose sort of thought that the Patriots were right. She wanted freedom, and she thought that the country should have it, also. She was shocked because of the awful thing that they were going to do to get freedom. Rose knew that she should warn her father. What if he got killed? That was such a horrible thought that Rose shivered, despite the warm air. What if she did tell her father and then the Patriots lost all of the battles and the colonies never got free?

"Why did I eavesdrop on them? It just made things worse," whispered Rose to herself. She was very confused. Should she tell her mother? Oh no, another decision! That night Rose avoided questions from her worried mother and went straight to her room to think about what she had done and what she should do.

That night and the next day, Rose thought and thought. Rose thought that the Patriots were right in thinking that the colonies should have freedom. But then there was Father. What if Rose caused him to die by not telling him that the Patriots were planning an attack?

Mrs. Winters knew that something was on Rose's mind, but despite all of her questions she couldn't get anything out of her. The next day, Rose decided to tell her mother about all of the news that she had heard at the Parkers' house. It all spilled out and when Rose was done, she knew what she had to do. Rose asked her mother if she could have one piece of her violet-scented stationery to write to her father.

Rose explained the situation to him the best she could. When she was done, Rose's mother gave it to the man who was delivering mail to the Tories. Rose felt good and her mother could rest in peace because she now knew what was bothering her daughter.

That evening Rose felt so good that she made a pincushion for her mother and played with Elizabeth. Rose knew that she had done the right thing.

Sarah White
Grade 6
Woodbury School
Shaker Heights, Ohio

Before you read on, stop to consider the very real strengths of this story. Take out a piece of paper and make notes for yourself or discuss the story with others in your workshop. Then, after you have considered the strengths of "Rose's War" thoroughly, ask yourself how this story might be improved. If you were revising it, where would you begin?

When you have done that, read on to see how my comments compare with your own. If your list is different from mine, that is fine. Mine doesn't cover every possible point. But think about my comments, too.

"Rose's War" is complex and believable, and it deals with an important issue in a realistic way. The story focuses closely on Rose's problem from beginning to end. She has two problems actually, but one leads smoothly into the other. Rose wants more freedom than girls were given in her time, and she wants her country to have freedom, too, despite the fact that her parents are Tories. And the dilemma she stumbles into by the end—knowing the details of an ambush in which her own father could be caught—is a powerful one.

The author, Sarah, is particularly effective at weaving historical details into the narrative without stopping the story for explanations, both personal and general. We learn about the political significance of being invited

167

for hot chocolate (not tea) when Rose declines to tell her mother that part of the invitation. We understand the implications of the divisions in the community when she stumbles into the Patriots' picnic. We find out that Rose is a girl with a mind of her own—in a time that didn't value such a trait—when the story opens with her being in trouble with the cook over dawdling. Sarah is even successful in creating dialogue that sounds as though it came out of the Revolutionary War era—"I'll be there in a heartbeat"—and that is a difficult feat, indeed.

Sarah uses description well, too, weaving it in throughout the forward-moving action. She creates a believable and immensely likable character in Rose. And with a couple of small exceptions when Sarah slips and tells us what Rose's mother is thinking, the author remains solidly in Rose's point of view. Sarah's mastery of these techniques is impressive.

As is almost always the case, however, there are layers to this story that haven't been explored yet. For one thing, we can almost see the writer wearing down as the story moves on, growing a bit tired. (This is one good reason why developing writers do well to stay with shorter stories. Most have difficulty sustaining a longer piece without, eventually, hurrying to be done.)

While the opening scenes are played out, using dialogue and description and skillfully revealing Rose's thoughts and feelings, later scenes tend to be summarized, told to us by the narrator. The scene in which Rose overhears the Patriot soldiers' plan, for instance, should be one of the most important in the story, but it is summarized. Neither Rose nor the reader gets a chance to feel the significance of what is happening.

As always, further fine-tuning could be done with language, too. For instance, "Rose was having the time of her life" is a cliché and adds little to our experience of Rose's time with Lucy. Perhaps you can find other places where the language could be refined further.

Most important, though, Rose's crucial decision is made without enough struggle. The conflict the author has set up is complex and fascinating. Can Rose go against her own convictions and against what she thinks is best for her country in order to protect her beloved father? Her decision to do so, while believable, comes too easily. Something more needs to happen in this story. Rose needs to become involved in some kind of strong action that will, finally, make her decision clear.

Perhaps Rose herself, independent young woman that she is, should decide to go to the front to contact her father in person. Or she might try to find a way to lure him home so he, at least, will be protected from the massacre without the Patriots' cause being put in jeopardy. Or you might be able to think of some other way to end the story.

The author herself may want to return to this story and explore these further layers. Or perhaps "Rose's War" was a product of another time in Sarah's life, and she no longer has the desire to embark on such deep revisions. To be successful fiction writers, we *must* learn to revise. But some stories are written, shared with our friends, then put aside without all the effort of revision. What matters is that we use each story to discover both our unique strengths and the techniques we need to develop more fully as writers. Then we move on and apply these techniques to fresh material.

As I mentioned in the beginning, even though you can't bring your own stories to this book for comments, you can take what you have discovered here back to your own work and revise. When you have learned how to revise, how to move your stories through many layers, making them deeper, stronger, truer to your own convictions, you will be a writer indeed.

CHAPTER 12

Enjoy!

*I*n *What's Your Story? A Young Person's Guide to Writing Fiction,* I made one point again and again, and I return to it now. There is only one good reason for writing stories. That is because you love doing it. As we've seen, fiction writing is a complex task. It's the kind of task you will have to work at for many years before you can even think of trying to compete with professionals for publication. (I can assure you, professional writers find it difficult to compete with one another for publication, too!)

But if you enjoy writing stories, I hope you will go on doing it. And doing it and doing it and doing it. Publication may, indeed, be your long-term goal. But it is the pleasure we writers take in the process that keeps us at our desks.

Your stories will, almost inevitably, grow as you do. And I hope seeing this work by other young writers has encouraged you in your writing and given you insights into ways in which you can make your own stories stronger.

To conclude, I give you two more stories by young writers without any intruding comments of my own.

These stories are especially effective. Read and enjoy. Take note of what makes them work so well.

Neither is perfect, however. Think about suggestions you might make for improvement. Do you understand the characters' motivations, for instance? Is the authors' language effective? Are any points confusing? Do you find yourself feeling with the main character? Are the endings satisfying?

Mutiny

"Riggers! Hop to it!" Captain Herschwitz's commanding voice reverberated throughout the cabin. "We're sailing right into the middle of a nova storm! Out of bed, you sluggards!"

As the chains retracted from our cold, sore limbs, I joined a handful of Light Riggers stumbling out of stiff, uncomfortable cots. Finally we gained our footing, moaning and groaning, only to be thrown to the deck by a tremendous rocking. I struggled to my feet, slowly adapting to the ship's violent shaking. Looking about the room, I saw Teor, the only other Rigger still standing.

"Is now the time?" he asked me, whispering.

Without hesitation, I nodded. "Yes. Yes, it is. Wake the others after I pass us through the storm, Teor. I will return soon, with . . ."

"RIGGERS!!!"

"What's our current speed, Captain?" I shouted quickly, straining to be heard over the noise of the storm's buffeting.

"Way too slow! We'll get stuck in the middle of this blasted maelstrom!" came the answer from the hulking Captain.

I ran up to the heavy door which separated the crew's cabin from the main deck and tapped the Request-to-Leave-Cabin button. Entering the Light Riggers' cabin was easy, but leaving required help from the outside. The door slid open hastily, as if it couldn't open fast enough for the person in charge.

I timed the swaying of the ship and hurled myself up the steps to the deck, just in time to be hit by a rolling storage barrel. Ignoring the pain of my injured, throbbing leg, I tried to reach the Captain. This time I succeeded.

The dark scoundrel, wobbling his way along the far deck, roared at me. "Took long enough! Get to the sails, Rigger!"

I sprinted up the steel ropes of the ship and jumped into the "crow's nest." Don't ask me what a crow is. I think it was an ancient god of sailing, but I'm not sure. The crow's nest of the Light-Rigged ship is its command center. Through a very complex computerized system, the Captain alters the ship's course only with the help of the Riggers. As I firmly grasped the controls, I once again marveled at the power of the forces I felt surging through me.

Following a short, sharp blast of light, seen only by astronomers and very, very lucky sailors, the first real warning of an incoming nova storm arrived. Composed of light gases blown off a star during the initial stages of an exploding nova, these intensive solar winds were sweeping the skies. The buffeting we had just experienced was caused by these winds, rapidly worsening as we approached the center of the storm. Large chunks of flaming gas would soon be tearing through space putting us in greater danger of collision. Greater danger than if we were to fly through an

173

asteroid belt at the speed of light, less than half our average velocity.

The difficulty in getting out of the solar wind lay in the steering. If I did not pilot the ship just so, the wind would flip us all into such a wild spin that it would take the combined skills of a Light Ship's regular complement of twenty-four Light Riggers to stabilize us. My ship, the Battle-axe, had seventeen Light Riggers. The manpower was kept limited so that the Captain would have no difficulty in controlling his crew.

I am a highly skilled Rigger—still, it took a tremendous effort of speedy manipulation before I was able to adjust the ship's positional direction perfectly. My hands moved in a beautifully orchestrated pattern, using the tools at my fingertips to save us all from utter destruction. I laughed at the irony—a slave saving the world!

After safely piloting the ship out of the area, I adjusted the engines and altitude to compensate for our sudden detour. I then climbed out of the nest and across the rigging to a batch of empty solar-cell blocks. Normally such blocks held one solar cell each, but these held much greater treasures. Opening the box-like containers one by one, I found what I wanted. I quickly took out six of the precious contraband, smiled, and climbed down to the Rigger cabin.

By the time I dropped from the rigging and slipped into the crew's cabin, my fourteen enlisted Light Riggers were all awake and waiting for me. Immediately, I was beset with questions from my excited recruits.

"Well? Did you get them? Where are they? Do you really think we can win? Were you seen?"

I waved down their jabbering. "Please, brother-friends. I have them here, under my grav belt. We will now win with ease. And please, do not insult me. Of course, I was not seen."

I kept one weapon for myself and distributed the other five to the mates I felt to be the most worthy. Trustworthy, that is. They checked their newly acquired armaments thoroughly and found them to be quite satisfactory.

"Now is the time we shall release ourselves from our bonds," I said at last. "Are we all prepared for what is to come?"

A few waved religious symbols in the air and all vigorously assented. Brontith began humming a victory song. Very soon the Captain would call us updeck to berate us for our "lazy" and "yellow-bellied" performance during the storm. As on cue, the door slid open and a loud, harsh voice interrupted our conference.

"Riggers! Get on deck! Captain's orders! Move it!"

It was First Mate Erdyhm, the Captain's number-one bully boy. Lucky for us he stayed updeck. The three traitorous Light Riggers, whom we had tied up in their beds, were plain to see. I looked at each of my brother-friends in turn and nodded.

"Now."

We rushed up the steps as one. Erdyhm was the first to fall prey to our attack, I noted with satisfaction. Then Second Mate Raellor, a worse thug than Erdyhm, went down, gaping up at us from the communications board. That left the Captain himself and his robotic guard. Although there were only ten small androids, they were well equipped with super-accelerated reflexes and heightened strength. But the tool of surprise is a great one, indeed, and three of the guards collapsed before they could employ their weapons, great heavy, club-like devices at the end of their multiple telescoping arms. Finally, the other seven robots joined the fray, ending our monopolized offensive.

To be violent is truly against our species' nature, civilized as we are, very unlike the Captain and his barbaric ilk. Yet we Light Riggers performed well in the midst of battle. The ferocity and viciousness displayed were absolutely inspiring. Long-forgotten warriors' cries exploded from our lips as we engaged in that which had been forbidden for centuries—mutiny, rebellion, violence. As child-mates we were raised to believe violence was evil. But we had also been taught that slavery, too, was evil. And so we fought to the death for our own freedom, for our own rule.

The machines lay at our feet, broken, twisted, destroyed. Yet also at our feet lay five of our dedicated comrades. Two Light Riggers were killed by the robotic guard, and three others had been thrown into that fatal paroxysmic condition brought about by a hand phaser, specifically the Captain's phaser.

Suddenly Mdontr-deRoth fell to his knees beside me with a cry, his face contorting in pain, his chest aglow with phaser energy. The second discharge into his body was largely wasted, as his neural passageways had already been basically annihilated by the first. The Captain brought his phaser to bear on the rest of us, laughing.

"Anyone want some more?" he snarled. "Back! Back, you quivering bunch of brainless scum! Ya! You don't want to feel my bite, do you, you trembling little corpses? Ha! Back to your cages, you animals! Get in your cabin, I say!"

I stood my ground and looked him hard in the eye. I saw that now it was he who trembled. This action was

176

a calculated risk, knowing that it would take several moments to re-energize, aim, and fire a hand phaser after a double shot. I had decreed earlier that the Captain was to be my personal target, and now was my chance. I spoke quickly, the words issuing forth in a tense proclamation of hatred and anger.

"We are not your slaves any more, Herschwitz. You are not Captain—I am! And now, justice!"

I had wanted to say something profound, more prophetic: "No more shall we toil under your harsh tyranny, your evil autocracy, for now we control our own destiny!" But I had too little time and too much hate. Before the Captain—that is, Herschwitz—could lift his phaser and cut me down in my glory, I raised my weapon and fired.

Later I was in the Captain's quarters where a soft whooshing sound, followed by a loud clanging, reached my ears through the bulkhead. I recognized what was happening instantly. Another ship was locking onto our airlock and preparing to board! Just as I moved to leave, Otil-amDherf, my second-in-command, burst into the room, and we collided.

"AmDherf!" I said. "What . . . ?"

"Freedom Police! And they want to talk to the Captain!"

I breathed a sigh of relief. "Is that all? I can handle them!"

The trio of Belundrian Freedom Police stood still in the center of the greeting chamber, their two mechanized attendants leaning against the wall opposite the door. I walked directly to the tallest Police-person with the largest badge. He appeared to be in charge.

Before I could utter a single word of greeting, he

bowed and spoke. "Hello, brother-stranger. My name is Nrdex, sergeant, and I come in search of a criminal. His name is Herschwitz, and he is known to be captain of this vessel, the Lightship Battle-axe."

"He is no longer captain of this vessel, brother-stranger," I said calmly, almost formally. "I am now captain."

All three Police-persons raised their eye-ridges in surprise.

"Is the transaction of the captainship public?" asked the smallest of the three.

"Yes, nearly a full Galactic hour ago," I said. "It seems Captain Herschwitz had been treating his Light Riggers despicably, treating us as impotent slaves. Often we were chained and beaten, locked into our cots at night, and confined to cramped quarters at all times. Freedom simply became a dream to us. Finally, we fought back. I led my fellow Light Riggers to victory in what amazingly was a peaceful mutiny. We captured the Captain and his two partners with minimal violence. Now I lead through the Right of Legal Mutiny. If you wish to take possession of our prisoners, I will gladly rid myself of their noxious presence."

The Freedom Police reacted perfectly to my little speech, gasping in shock and horror at the Captain's cruelty and sighing in relief that the rebellion had been accomplished peacefully.

Nrdex smiled happily and said, "Thank you, brother-stranger! We are very pleased with these events. We had originally been concerned that force might prove to be necessary in capturing these men, but your actions have alleviated these fears completely. Yes, we do wish to take your prisoners into containment. Thank you!"

I echoed his grin and motioned to Otil-amDherf, the only other Light Rigger in the room.

"Yes, brother-sir?"

"Go and get the prisoners and bring them here immediately. Guard them well."

His eye-ridges lifted, and his hand lightly tapped his upper leg. I shook my head no, answering the unasked. The Freedom Police were not to know of our weapons. They would not understand our need.

"Immediately, brother-sir!" He left in haste.

After a few minutes of small-talk between the new Captain and the Freedom Police, amDherf returned with the prisoners, unconscious and on anti-grav stretchers. I thanked amDherf and Ryfnnej, his guard, and turned the comatose prisoners over to the Police. The two functionaries took the stretchers away, the Freedom Police following. Nrdex moved to leave with them, but I held up a restraining hand.

"Please, hold a moment, sergeant," I said.

"Yes?" Nrdex paused, waiting. "I need to leave soon, brother-stranger."

"Yes, I understand. I merely wish to ask you about Captain Herschwitz. Could you tell me . . . with what crime was he charged? It may be of some importance to me and my crew."

"Ah, that is classified infor . . ." I shook his hand, clinking the heavy coins into his palm. "I mean, of course, I can, brother-stranger! He is charged with a very heinous crime as all peace-loving people of the Galaxy would agree—that is, of course, the theft and smuggling of illegal weapons. Herschwitz is suspected to have used empty solar cell blocks to smuggle hand phasers, which he then sold to evil, violence-loving mercenary-fiends."

"Truly!" I exclaimed, taken aback. "I had thought the Captain bad, but never would I have suspected . . . ! Ah, well, I've always felt all human beings were villainous, contemptible savages."

Nrdex smiled his agreement.

I continued. "Gladly might I aid you in your search for evidence, but we have not found any such hidden weaponry aboard the ship. I will make certain of this, however, and contact you if, indeed, we find something. Thank you, brother-friend. You have been a great help. For this I salute you and call you brother-friend."

Nrdex's two mouths registered surprise and then curled up into two grins. He reciprocated my salute, saying, "And I, you, brother-friend." Quickly then he left, his four arms waving a cheerful good bye.

"Finally," gasped amDherf.

"I thought they'd never leave," sighed Ryfnnej.

"We need not fear any police force for a long, long time," I said, studying the trigger of my newly acquired and quite illegal hand phaser. It really was a marvelous piece of work.

I looked up at my crew of pirates.

"They'll never suspect us now."

The roar of universal domination thundered in my ears, deafening me to the reply of my companions.

Joseph V. L. Cook
Grade 11
Bloomington High School
Bloomington, Illinois

And a story of a very different type:

180

A *Tale of Two Kitties*

The fish dangled, dancing in front of my eyes. "I'm gonna get it, I'm gonna get it!" I stalked and pounced, just missing the taunting fish. "Ah shucks, missed it by a whisker." I slunk around the table peeking through the legs, daring the fish to come closer. But the Bearded One had dropped the toy.

"Have you noticed that you never catch the fish, Rajah?" Jasmine teased me and grinned.

Discouraged, I lay down.

"Fine, be a grumpy cat then," Jasmine said.

Oh good, I thought, *the Bearded One is coming back.* I pranced, meowing, "Let's play some more."

The Bearded One sighed, trying to get the weight off his shoulders. "Oh, Rajah. I'm too tired to play any longer," he said.

I looked deep into his dark eyes and didn't see any flicker of happiness. "Come here, Jasmine," I said. "The Bearded One needs some love."

We both jumped into his lap and purred as we licked the wool of his suit. He smiled and caressed my neck.

I ran back to the silly fish and took it to the Bearded One in my mouth. He smiled again and made the fish come alive. Even Jasmine got into this game. We all forgot about the Bearded One's problems and chased after the multi-colored fish.

But it wasn't long before Jasmine mumbled, "Oh, I hate this stupid stuffed . . . fish," and she lay down once more.

181

The Bearded One's smile faded.

Jasmine and I gave each other a knowing look. We'd both seen his loneliness before. The first time was when his love died, the One of Sunshine Hair. She was as beautiful and sweet as a summer's flower. Even when the Bearded One came home tired or discouraged, the One of Sunshine Hair could make him happy again with a flip of her lustrous hair. I wished I could do that.

I snuggled in my friend's arms, but the deep sorrow did not disappear from his face. As I jumped down from the ripped and ragged couch, I decided I just had to find someone who could make the Bearded One purely happy.

Jasmine stretched and came over to me. "Jasmine, his eyes scare me," I said.

"Why?"

"There's death in there. We need to find him a true love. Maybe then he won't be so sad, and he'll learn to live again."

"It's impossible," Jasmine replied. "Who is good enough for the Bearded One?"

I stumbled into the kitchen, trying to think of somebody.

Jasmine followed me, biting on a morsel of cat food, coughing it right back out. "Yuck! I wish the Bearded One would get new food. This stuff isn't even good enough for that toy fish!"

I sighed. Jasmine's grumbling was so familiar it comforted me in hard times. "Good night, my shimmering cloud." I yawned and finally fell asleep, hearing the loving voice of the One of Sunshine Hair when she used to fill our bowls with fresh food.

The next day, I watched the sun gliding up the silky

sky. "Wake up, Jasmine. It's time to wake up our friend!"

We climbed the stairs to the Bearded One's bedroom, Jasmine whimpering all the way about the steps being so tall. I jumped onto his sagging bed, but since Jasmine can't jump, she just meowed on the floor to help wake him up.

"Time to wake up, my friend," I purred.

He opened his sunken eyes. "Good morning," he said. "I love you, Rajah, my tiger."

Jasmine gave a little whimper. "Of course, I love you, too, little one."

I smiled, licking the stubble on his neck.

The Bearded One put on a suit for work. "I'll see you kitties at noon after I take care of some business," he said with not very much enthusiasm. I meowed at the door to the outside world for several minutes after the Bearded One left.

"Jasmine?" I explored and found her already napping. I shook my head and walked over to her. "Jasmine."

She opened her foggy eyes.

"You're all dirty again." She wasn't really, but I wanted to give her some loving licks.

"Okay," I said, "we're going to try this jumping thing one more time."

"No, Rajah! I've never jumped, and I never will. So give it up." She stayed stubbornly on the floor.

"Come on!"

Finally Jasmine got up, scowling all the way.

"Okay . . . no, push down on all four paws," I instructed. "Feel the tension from your claws to the tip of your tail. Twitch your tail-end until you feel the bounding energy pressing your paws, then spring!" I

183

jumped high in the air. It was one of my better efforts, which of course just made Jasmine's discouraged look deepen. "Jasmine, nobody can leap with that attitude."

"Fine, I'll try." She swished her whole back end, clawing the floor with the look of a bull. After exhausting and useless minutes of this, Jasmine only succeeded in lifting her front end up and tumbling backwards. "Well, I sure learned a lot. Gee, thanks, Rajah."

After napping for a couple of hours, I heard the whole neighborhood start to bark. That noise could mean only one thing, the woman who feeds the house with letters was here. "Jasmine! I thought of somebody for the Bearded One!"

"Who are you talking about?" Then I saw a knowing look spring to Jasmine's face as she heard the dogs barking. "That friendly woman could take the loneliness away from anyone. She's a giver of smiles."

I agreed. She always sent Jasmine and me many loving smiles and waves from outside as we purred against the windows. She was perfect for our friend. "The Bearded One and Giver of Smiles have to meet," I said. "I just know she can make his sorrow disappear."

"But how can we get her inside the house?" Jasmine asked.

"I've got an idea, listen." I told her my plan.

"I love it!" Jasmine's whole body started to quiver.

Just as the Giver of Smiles walked up to the porch, Jasmine leaped with all her energy into the air, up onto the desk next to where the letters come into the house.

I was so shocked and thrilled, I almost forgot about the plan. "Jasmine! You did it. You jumped!"

"Of course, I did. I knew I could all along. I just

184

didn't feel like it before." Jasmine pranced all over the desk.

"Okay, here come the letters," I said excitedly. "Let's start the plan." I nudged open the little wooden door where the letters come in and Jasmine stuck in her paw. I could feel the soft pads in my own front paw cringe in sympathy. I asked, "Are you sure this doesn't hurt?" She gave me a reassuring nod. "Okay, start meowing!"

Jasmine started to wail and cry to get the attention of the Giver of Smiles. It worked. She dropped her bag full of letters and tried opening the front door to see what was wrong. Since the Bearded One never locks the door, it opened easily.

"Hello?" the Giver of Smiles cried out. "Is anyone here?" What she saw was a little white cat acting all hurt and helpless, so she rescued Jasmine who immediately started to purr in her arms.

Meanwhile, I wove in and out between her ankles, meowing. The Giver of Smiles reached down to stroke my neck, right on the special place only the One of Sunshine Hair knew.

The door creaked open once again, but this time it was the Bearded One who came. He had this surprised look on his face, but soon that disappeared.

"Someone in here needed my help," said the Giver of Smiles. The tenderness in her face filled our house. Jasmine slid down from her arms and sat by me.

The Bearded One glanced at us and then stared at our new friend and nodded. All the stress and loneliness washed away, and a look that had been locked up came over him.

I touched Jasmine with my nose. "Well, my shimmering cloud, we did it."

"Together," Jasmine added and then started licking me. "Rajah, this time it's your coat that's dirty. Allow me."

Jessica Guernsey
Grade 9
Central High School
St. Paul, Minnesota

I hope the process of reading and workshopping the stories of other young writers has encouraged you and increased your understanding of fiction-writing techniques. Now, it's time to turn back to your own stories . . . with renewed pleasure.

Young Authors' Biographies

Beth Badger ("Future House," p. 145)
What I mainly use my writing for is to make people laugh and to escape reality. What usually happens is an idea pops into my mind after I see or hear something. I chuckle about it a little and write it down.

Alder Brannin (untitled excerpt, p. 9)
My name is Alder Melora Whistler Brannin. The alder is a kind of tree that grows along streams. I have always loved to read, fiction mostly. I have found that reading has helped me to expand my vocabulary, and writing has helped me to visualize the stories that I read more vividly.

Sophie Calderon ("Alone," p. 118)
The only time I write stories is when it's a school assignment. In order for me to have fun with writing stories, I try to connect it with reading stories. When I write I try not to know what's going to happen next in my stories, like you don't know what's going to happen next when reading a book. As I get older, story writing

assignments are given less, so I don't write as much, but I still sometimes create plots in my head.

Christina Capecchi ("Holly Christmas Mission," excerpt, p. 32)

As a preschooler, I illustrated my first book, *Mary the Monkey*. I've enjoyed writing ever since! In 1993 I represented my elementary school at a Young Authors' Conference where I heard featured speaker Marion Dane Bauer and bought her book *What's Your Story?* I have won first place in both national and local writing contests, and I am active in sports, music, and writing.

Jenna Carlson ("A Walk in the Park," p. 56)

I always used to badger my parents into telling stories of their growing-up years and into reading me stories, too. I was also forever telling stories as a child. I guess I never really grew up. Language has always been my passion, and that passion has led me to begin writing my stories down.

Joseph V. L. Cook ("Mutiny," p.172)

Always I have dreamt "impossible dreams." I won my first literary award at the age of five when I illustrated my yearnings to become a horn-honking seal. In junior high I aspired to be Isaac Asimov, extensively writing science fiction and space travel textbooks. Today I study aerospace engineering at Cal-Tech with plans to work at NASA's Jet Propulsion Lab. Dreams do come true. Who knows? You might find my signature written in tomorrow's stardust.

Kasi DeLaPorte ("Friends Forever," p. 89)

I was born on December 9, 1983. I like to draw, write, read, and play games on the computer, and I take jazz dancing. When I grow up I want to be an author/illustrator, a lawyer, or a judge.

Christen DiPetrillo ("Baseball or Girls' Softball," excerpt, p. 67)

Besides writing, I have many other interests. I play baseball for Kittatinny Little League (Majors). I'm also involved with football and wrestling, cheerleading, and Girl Scouts. I recently won an award for the essay contest at our school for Earth Day. I have also recently been presented the Chief School Administrators' Round Table Award for the state of New Jersey.

Jessica Guernsey ("A Tale of Two Kitties," p. 181)

I have grown up with writing. My mother is a writer, and she taught me how to use words in exciting and expressive ways. I have been sending my stories and poems to contests since I was seven years old, when I won a trip to New York for my entire family with my essay about the Statue of Liberty.

Jamey Hamilton ("Emergency!" p. 51)

In addition to writing, I enjoy writing computer programs, swimming, and baseball. When I grow up I plan to attend Harvard Medical School.

Andrew Hand (untitled excerpt, p.126)

I grew up with two older brothers who loved torturing me. I had to use my small size to get away from them. My mother supported us all on a tight budget until she graduated from college and became a minister. In spite of being a pastor's son, I manage to live a normal life. I enjoy reading the finest books and usually only write for assignments. I enjoy sports and playing with my dog.

Jessica Hermo ("The Proving Project," p. 96)
I have been writing stories since second grade. I enjoy cheerleading, gymnastics, and ballet. I would like to be a teacher when I grow up and write stories in my spare time.

Nathan David Hunt ("One Shot," p. 132)
Growing up with two older brothers, I quickly developed a love for competitive sports reflected today in my membership on my high school basketball team and hitting the tennis courts and golf courses with my friends. I love to read, listen to soft music, travel, and spend time with my friends and my brothers. Writing comes as a joy I share from my own wealth of experience.

Amy Jackson ("Daddy's Little Girl," excerpt, p. 12)
Writing has always been a love of mine, but poems were the only things I had ever written. When I was given an assignment to write a short story, I thought that it might be a good way to broaden my writing horizons. It certainly was.

Jason Jaeger ("A Measly Five Dollars," p. 23)
The activities I enjoy most are skiing, Rollerblading, biking, and spending time with my friends. I really don't like writing for school papers and assignments. I like to write when it is for me, when I'm in the mood.

Jennifer Lee ("The Legend of Vampire Valley," p. 39)

I love gymnastics, reading, and writing. One of my goals is to write a suspense novel in poetry. One unique thing about me is that I can remember quotes and phrases, which I weave into my stories.

Mark A. Lopez ("The Never-Ending Game," p. 69)

My favorite kind of writing is action writing. I like to write stories that have adventure in them. Most of the stories I write for school have to do with an experience I've had before, and I just change it and make it more exciting. Ever since I started writing, I've always enjoyed it and I know I always will.

Marisa Martinson ("Lean on Me," p. 77)

I spent my first three years with my parents in the tropical paradise of Hawaii. After moving to Minnesota, I found the cold, yet beautiful winters to be fascinating. Experiencing a blizzard firsthand inspired my writing of "Lean on Me." My passion for writing was actually kindled at a very early age when a book that I wrote and illustrated was displayed at a writers' fair.

Andrew Nichols ("Forgiveness," p. 59)

I enjoy writing very much. I write everything from poetry to essays and research papers. One of my favorite subjects is human turmoil, how something affects a person or persons and how they deal with it. I plan to continue writing as long as God sees fit to give me the ability to.

Derek J. Oberg ("Frank and the Grizzly," p. 102)

I am very interested in the outdoors, and I enjoy canoeing, fishing, biking, and target shooting. I run track and play basketball and soccer. As a beginning writer I enjoy writing about the things I know and in which I participate.

Tina Overmyer (untitled excerpt, p. 43)

I am a girl trying to find myself. I express my biggest fears and anger as well as love through my writing. Since grade school I've enjoyed writing stories, poems, and (my personal favorites) songs. I enjoy writing because there are no wrong answers and I'm in control of the entire writing.

Brooke Roberts (untitled excerpt, p. 4)

I am sixteen years old and have been homeschooling for six years. I spend a lot of time writing in my journal or sketching out short stories. I do my best writing in my room with loud music in the background. This is my first published story.

Laura Rogers ("How I Became a Hero," excerpt, p. 127)

My writing is like my mirror. One side is reality, and reflected in the mirror is that reality backwards. In my story Darwin is the opposite of the expected because he thinks he's a cat. Robert Frost did the same. He wanted to write about choices, and his "mirror" showed him "The Road Not Taken."

Jaclyn Nicole Shaw ("The Best Birthday Present," p. 137)

I have always loved to write stories and poems. I usually get an idea for a story and think about it for a while before trying to write it down. I like using the computer to write since my hand gets tired when I write with a pencil! I have written one book called *Go to Sleep, Mr. Moon*, which is my mom's favorite.

Anahid Thompson ("No Harm Will Come to Good," excerpt, p. 27)

I would really like to be a writer when I grow up. I have always enjoyed reading and have been inspired by the authors J. D. Salinger and John Steinbeck. I aspire to someday write stories as descriptive and provocative as theirs.

Suzanne Van Rijn ("A Visit with My Attic Friends," p. 86)

Before I was very capable of writing stories down on paper, I would narrate them into a tape recorder. At that age, I had no idea what a plot or theme was, but somehow my stories just developed on their own. Now that I'm older, I find it's *much* more difficult to write a story. Hardly anything comes naturally anymore, except, of course, my love of storytelling.

Amy Webster ("Anything for Staci," p. 109)

This is the first story I have ever published. I hope someday to become a recording artist and probably write a few novels for young adults.

Sarah White ("Rose's War," p. 154)

I have always enjoyed reading and writing, historical fiction being one of my favorite types of books. That is why I chose to set "Rose's War" during the Revolutionary War. I live with my parents, my sister, Lauren, and my brother, Alex. I enjoy playing sports, field hockey, lacrosse, and swimming being my favorites.

Gretchen Yancey ("The Air Pie," p. 16)

I write poetry and short stories in my free time. This story, which I wrote in twelfth grade, is my first story to be published, although I have won awards for my poetry. Many of my creations incorporate memories from my childhood or stories my mother, a storyteller, shared with me.

Annemarie Ziegler ("The Puppy Rescue," excerpt, p. 48)

I love reading books and writing stories. I especially like to write books about teenagers, stories I have gone through, am experiencing, or imagine myself or others going through. I love to write because it lets me get away and have something all to myself. I hope to continue writing, maybe as a hobby or as a career.

Authors Whose Photographs Appear on the Front of the Jacket

Top row, left to right: Mark A. Lopez, Annemarie Ziegler, Jennifer Lee, Andrew Nichols

Center row, left to right: Beth Badger, Jamey Hamilton, Christina Capecchi, Jason Jaeger

Bottom row, left to right: Nathan David Hunt, Amy Webster, Jessica Hermo, Andrew Hand

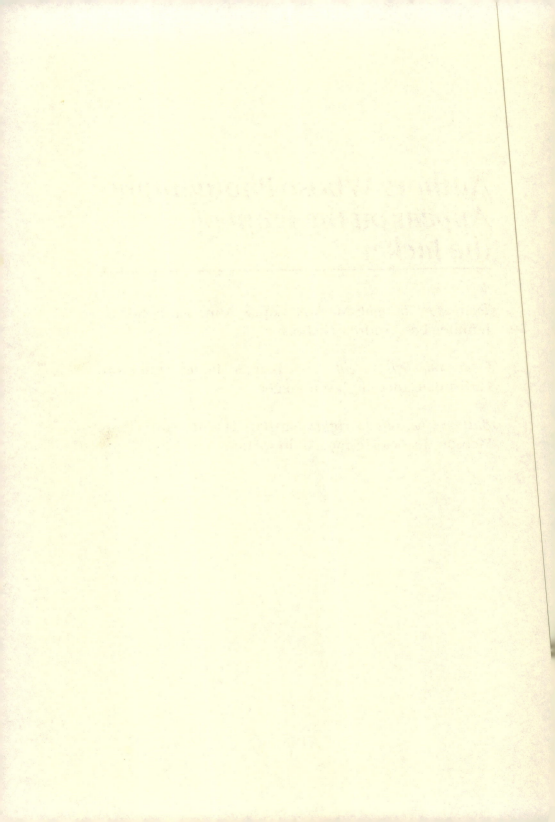